That Reminds Me
Of the Time....
Volume 3

An Anthology

By the

Arizona Highway Patrol
Arizona D.P.S.
Coalition of DPS Retirees, Inc.

Published by CLC Publishing, LLC.
Mustang, OK 73064

Printed in the United States of America

Cover Photo

The cover photo was taken at the only location in the United States where the corners of 4 states meet, Utah, Colorado, Arizona and New Mexico. The monument is located within the confines of the Navajo Indian Reservation and denotes the geographic location of the states where they meet. Each officer is standing within the round monument in the position his state occupies. Arizona DPS officer Andy Beck in tan uniform, Utah Highway Patrol in dark brown shirt, light brown trousers, Colorado State Patrol in Blue shirt, grey trousers, New Mexico State Police in Black with grey accents.

Coalition of DPS Retirees, Inc.

The Coalition of DPS Retirees proudly presents this book for your reading pleasure. It is comprised of true stories and experiences written and compiled by members and their families of our Coalition.

Colin Peabody, Chairman
Ed Felix, Vice Chairman
Norma Risch, Secretary
James Gentner, Comptroller
Ardith Hundley, Member Services

Acknowledgements

Colin Peabody, Paul Palmer, Heber John Davis, Louie Chaboya, John Fink, Dick Lewis, Ron Bruce, Bob Singer, Larry Scarber, Bob Ticer, Frank Glenn, Dennis McNulty, Alan Whitney, Greg Eavenson, Steve Gendler, TK Waddell, Richard Richardson, Roger Vanderpool, Doug Kluender, Bill Hansen, Bill Breen, Bill Rogers, Ron Cox, Charlie Ruiz, Jim Heflin, Harley Thompson, Ben Hancock, Darryl Mullins, Randy Strong, Rick Williams, Gil Duthie, Ralph Shartzer, Steve Hinderliter, Jim Bob Davis, Rick Ulrich, Gary Ciminski, John Underwood, Don Barcello, Tim Hughes, Steve Lump, Lee Patterson, Gay Anderson, Brian Frank, Johnny Sanchez, Dick Shafer, Heston Silbert

Dedication

Our previous books, That Reminds Me of The Time Vol 1 and 2, were dedicated to the men and women of the AHP/DPS. We would like to dedicate Vol 3 to the spouses and family of these officers. The men, women and children who stood behind these brave officers who daily faced the dangers of being a police officer.

It begins with, "We are being stationed where?" to "When will you be home?" or for the folks stationed in the far reaches of the state, "Can we take a trip to Phoenix, Flagstaff, Tucson or any place with a restaurant or movie theater?"

They watched each day as the patrol car pulled away from the house with mixed feelings of fear and pride. The children proud but unconcerned. They knew to give their officer space after a long shift when it was apparent that it had been rough day.

We have seen families sitting beside a flag draped coffin of their fallen officer. We watched them bravely try to hold back tears as the flag is slowly folded by the honor guard and then presented by the director. They hold and console the children during the helicopter fly over and the playing of taps.

To the families of all of our officers, we say thank you.

A Tribute To Our Law Enforcement Wives And Moms

By Colin Peabody #481

This was written on Mother’s Day, 2022 as a way of paying tribute to our long-suffering wives and moms.

We want to take a few moments to wish a very happy Mother's Day to all our Law Enforcement Moms, who sent their husbands off to their duties with a kiss and an I Love You, not knowing what the next hours or days would bring to their families. Those Moms who endured long hours while their husband worked a dangerous job, investigating accidents, arresting dangerous individuals, conducting long investigations, fighting harsh weather, dust storms, blizzards, torrential rains and flooding, not knowing what their man was doing, where he was or when he would be home. Those Moms who answered the phone at 3 in the morning to a call from the AHP Dispatcher, calling to send her sleeping husband off to some call, Moms who got the kids up, fixed their lunches, sent them off to school, maybe having to tend to family livestock, feeding and maybe milking a cow, hooking up a horse trailer to the pickup to help rescue some four legged animals belonging to someone she doesn't know, because the dispatcher called and said her husband wanted her to do that; sitting with other patrol wives outside an emergency room with the wife of an officer injured in the line of duty or worse, and knowing their husbands were still out there looking for the person or persons responsible for causing them to be there together comforting each other, worried about their own husband's safety; welcoming a stranger or a family at their door because her husband said they had no place to go or nothing to eat after a terrible event occurred to them.

These Moms endured so much to support their patrol husbands, often in far out duty stations where the closest phone was across the road at a gas station or on a telephone phone half a mile away, miles away from grocery stores and medical help, which may have been in a neighboring state, living in a cramped and often run down aluminum 14' by 60' box costing $25 a month, parked in a state yard or near a gas station because that was the only housing available, or even in what had once been a chicken coop converted into a small apartment in a small town on old Route 66. They relied on other patrol wives for support and even grocery runs to the store 50-60 miles or more away. They looked out for each other's kids as if they were their own.

Why did they endure this? Because they loved their husbands, they were strong young women raised by mothers who had endured the Depression of the 1930s, World War II, Korea and other difficult times in the mid-20th century. In today's world, when the cable goes out and no internet or Wi-Fi for more than a few minutes, the battery on our cell phone goes dead, we are inconvenienced because this is what we have become used to.

But every so often, we need to reflect back on what the patrol wives over the past 90 years have endured without those modern conveniences in THEIR service to the citizens of the State of Arizona and pay tribute to them.

And so I say to the Moms of the AHP/DPS family:

HAPPY MOTHER'S DAY! Because we couldn't have done it without you! God Bless you all!

INTRODUCTION

When the Covid pandemic had everyone holed up in their homes I contacted Colin Peabody, Chairman of the Coalition of Department of Public Safety Retirees and suggested that we request our retirees to submit stories about their careers. Little did I know what would happen next.

Colin e-mailed CDPSR members, and they responded with great stories. Colin would then send these stories out to everyone to enjoy. It wasn't long before people began saying, you need to make these stories into a book.

Colin and I took these stories and That Reminds Me Of The Time was soon a book of 355 pages. It included stories about the beginnings of our department along with stories that made you laugh and a few that brought tears.

We thought this was a great accomplishment that our retirees made possible. But the stories kept coming and it wasn't long before we had a book two and now, we have here, book 3.

I can't say enough about the fantastic retirees of AHP/DPS. As a young kid growing up in Gila Bend, I was always around Arizona Highway Patrolmen. Some lived at the highway department yard where I lived and some just stopped by the house on their way through town. These men were my heroes. I never once in a million years thought that someday I would work with these heroes and that later I would be interviewing them or would receive stories about their careers that would result in a book.

During my 40 years with the department as both a sworn and a civilian employee I have worked with or known the most honorable and dedicated people I have ever known, some legends and some just plain ole characters. But they all had a great love for the department which made us a close knit, united group.

When assigned to the video unit I had the opportunity to travel the state, literally from border to border. No matter where I went, the camaraderie and dedication were very evident. On some assignments I may work with an officer in a remote area of the state for just a few hours, but many times it resulted in a close friendship that lasts to this day.

I could go on and on about our retirees but that would be another book. Read on and you will see what I am talking about. Let me end by saying thank you to all retirees who gave me the opportunity and their trust to put these books together.

This is your book. Thank you.

Paul Palmer #342

As I look at the calendar, January 22, 2023, I reflect back on the last 55 years of my involvement with the Arizona Highway Patrol, which became the Arizona Department of Public Safety in July 1969, and of all the great friends I have gained in my various assignments, as a patrolman, sergeant, civilian employee and volunteer. Over those years, my family, friends and relatives have told me I should write a book. Well, I am not alone in hearing that sentiment expressed.

Over the past two decades serving as a Board Member and Chairman of the Coalition of DPS Retirees and as a volunteer with the AHP/DPS Heritage Museum, I have heard that same sentence more times than I can remember. I know all the folks who contributed to the two previous volumes of "That Reminds Me of The Time" and now Volume 3 in the series, have been given the opportunity to tell many of their stories without having to go through the tribulations of authoring a book and getting it published. Each volume has had more "authors" than the previous edition, which tells us there are more stories yet to be told. Paul Palmer and I have been good friends and worked together for many years. When we approached the Coalition with this book concept during the pandemic, the Board of the Coalition of DPS Retirees, Inc., saw the value in creating a written legacy of the dedicated employees of this great agency and now the stories can be read in the very unedited (well, maybe in a few instances!) words of the "authors". You can literally "hear" the author's voice as the story is related.

These stories can now be joined with a visit to the AHP/DPS Heritage Museum, located within the Headquarters building where those stories are brought to life with artifacts used, gathered and donated by our folks over the course of their careers. No visit to the Museum is complete without poring over the several hundred engraved, personalized bricks that line the walkway leading in and out of the Museum, a concept suggested by our former Director, Col. Heston Silbert. Each brick holds stories as we look back over the names we see, and we are "reminded of the times" and adventures we shared.

We hope you enjoy this volume as much as you have the other two.

Colin Peabody #481

I was born in South Bend, Indiana and moved to Arizona in 1934. We moved to Coolidge where I attended school. There were two Highway Patrolmen who would be at the school, Roger Gates and Clarence Tyra. They were sharp looking patrolmen and were well respected. They left an impression on me.

In 1954 I was working for a lumber company in Coolidge driving a truck hauling supplies between Coolidge and Phoenix. My wife had seen an article in the paper that said the Highway Patrol was hiring and a cadet class would soon start. This was after the Merit System was in place.

On June 1, 1954 I began the academy with 16 other men. Three additional men were scheduled to start the academy and were scheduled to arrive after about two and a half weeks into the school. The Highway Patrol was so short of officers that they shortened the academy to seven weeks and sent us out on OJT. When we got out on patrol, there were still fewer than 100 officers on the road. I started on the department making $325.00 a month with a $15.00 uniform allowance. Top pay was $362.50 after 3 years and after 10 years you got longevity pay. We worked 6 days a week.

I was sent to Wickenburg along with George Schuck who was also in my class. There were two officers in Wickenburg, Horbart Smith, and George Pemberton. Bill Hanger was in Yarnell and Bill Whitlow was in Wenden. Peso Dollar was in Salome.

After a month in Wickenburg I was assigned to Wittman. I found a house for rent in Morristown, only 10 miles away from Wittman for less money, but Capt. Dysart Murphy said no, that I had to live in Wittman. I don't know his reasoning, but you had better do what Capt. Murphy said.
He scared me to death!

They built a new house at the weigh station in Beardsley to replace the trailer there. A Highway Department employee had been living in the trailer as a caretaker and had retired. I asked Superintendent Hathaway if I could move into the house. He said he would check with the highway commissioner. I then said since they were paying $110 a month for security of the station, how about if I lived in the house free of rent to provide the security. He said he would ask the commissioner. Hathaway approved both requests and I lived in the house rent free for seven years.

I made Sergeant on July 1, 1961, and transferred to Gila Bend. I had a choice of Globe or Gila Bend, and I chose Gila Bend because I liked that district commander better. I spent 2 years, 15 days, 4 hours and 27 minutes in Gila Bend and was then transferred to Nogales. When I told my wife we were being transferred to Nogales she cried. I told her she hated the heat so what was wrong. She had never been to Nogales and she pictured a town of white plastered mud huts. It was August and we took a drive to Nogales and as we were being showed around a summer rainstorm blew in and she got so cold she had to borrow a sweater. She said anyplace in Arizona where you needed a sweater in August would be just fine.

I then transferred to Tucson in July 1 1969 and was later promoted to Lt in 1970. The department was housed in a building with the driver's license division. They had half the building, and we had the other half. One quarter was for patrol and one quarter for CI. Capt. LaPonsie was the CI Captain and Lt Dierking was the Lt over narcotics. The Highway Patrol commander, Capt. McCollum drew a line down the middle of the foyer. He said, this half is for the highway patrol and you CI S.O.B.s get the other half. Not a good start for welcoming the CI personnel to DPS!

I made Captain in Tucson in January 1971 and was then transferred to Phoenix. My first assignment in Phoenix was as administrative assistant to Col Robertson. He made sure that I knew that I was an administrative assistant, not assistant superintendent.

The department was a great department but when Vern Hoy from LAPD was selected as Director in Jan 1976 it was a dark time. Vern tried to make DPS into another LAPD. He was very hard to work with and every time you submitted paperwork to him, he would change it, writing in the margins and between the lines. This got so bad I suggested that I bring the officer responsible for submitting paperwork to him to his office and talk with him so he could get an idea of how he wanted things written. I took Lt Chandler up to Hoy's office with a paper that had been written seven times before. Hoy looked at it and began marking it up. Lt Chandler handed him the same paper he had previously corrected the way he wanted it and Hoy said, fine and Lt Chandler left. Hoy told me to never bring that officer to his office again.

Soon after Hoy arrived, he brought charges against some of the brass. Some people thought that I was behind the charges and were upset with me. That was the furthest thing from the truth. I told Hoy that these were honorable men and that if he felt there was no place for them in the department that he should just tell them so and that they would have retired. I told him, please don't go to the newspapers with this and smear the good name of this department. He rejected my request. I just happened to be assigned to a position where they thought I influenced Hoy. That has always bothered me.

Hoy brought three people from California to form an assessment center. The top twenty ranked men in the department were sent to the assessment center. We had to rank each other and the three men from California also ranked us. Hoy told me I came out #1 ranked by fellow officers and #1 by the assessment personnel. I was promoted to Lt Col in September 1976. Also promoted to Lt Col was Carroll Pennington, Ken Forgia and Larry Thompson. Bernie Flood, a civilian, was prompted and remained in Technical Communications.

Hoy asked me where I wanted to go, and I told him that I probably should go to an administrative position to broaden my knowledge. I really didn't want an admin job but thought it would be better for me. I was assigned to the Administration Division.

The new governor wanted to get rid of Hoy, but Hoy said he had one more year left on his contract. The governor
said that the first year of his appointment was temporarily filled by Col Robertson as acting director and that counted towards his 5-year appointment, so his 5-year term was now up. That is why we now have a 4-year term for director instead of 5 years.

I really enjoy the This Reminds Me Of The Time books. It brings back many memories, but I think some of the stories probably shouldn't have seen the light of day! The coalition is doing a great job of keeping everyone informed but I wish we could get some of the newer retirees to join the coalition. But I guess the Highway Patrol Association is having the same problem of recruiting officers. It is a different time, I guess.

I have been asked if it is true that I gave one of my badges to Make A Wish's Chris Grecius. I have kept that to myself for many years. I did give Chris one of my badges. I asked permission from Director Ralph Milstead, but he said no. Some of our badges in the past had turned up where they should not have been, and he did not want any badges given away that could wind up causing problems. I knew that Chris would be buried in full DPS uniform, and my badge would be buried with Chris, so I disobeyed Milstead and gave my badge to Chris.

I had a great career and I miss the people that I have worked with.

Ret Lt Colonel Dick Shafer #55

The venerable history and evolution of the Arizona Department of Public Safety is often denoted in transcendent titles. From Highway Patrolman, to Officer, to Arizona State Trooper. While the titles have changed over time, the Arizona Department of Public Safety continues to cascade much like the path carved by the Colorado River into Antelope Canyon. While the Colorado carved the path with water, the path of the Department of Public Safety is carved with the blood, sweat, courage, integrity, and honor of those past and those present. One needs to look no further than the public trust earned by the actions of the elite few who have filled the ranks of the "Silver-Tan." Day and night, freezing cold, simmering heat, the men and women of the Arizona Department of Public Safety provide the public hope and relief during the dire times life has to offer. While the remarkable people who formerly and currently comprise this agency consider themselves humble professionals, to the public, they are peace of mind.

The Arizona Department of Public Safety embraces and earned the public trust. Never is it taken for granted, nor is our history. Whether anecdotal, pictorial or tangible, the history of the Arizona Department of Public Safety must be cherished. This book is just one such example. In fact, "It Reminds Me of the Time." Please enjoy and embrace a bit of the honored history of the Arizona Department of Public Safety.

Col Heston Silbert #10000

DPS Director Ret

DO YOU REMEMBER

CDPSR Retirees

As you wrote and submitted stories, your memories began to pile up. Here are some of the things you brought back from the old days.

Badge numbers

1-499 Patrolman
500-599 Dispatchers
600-699 Radio Techs
700-799 Sergeants
800-899 Lieutenants
900 Captains and above
6000 Female employees
7000 Male employee

Some people with special ties to the department (political contact?) were given special numbers. Jimmy Minato for example was Adam 3

Blood runs

Eyeball runs

Prisoner transport

Hostesses on Trailways buses

Revolvers

Six round ammo holder

Change from wheel guns to automatics - choosing either 9mm or 45

Gates to enter or leave the compound were opened and closed by a dispatcher. The code was 105 to open and 106 to close

Long wooden batons

Ike jackets

Real leather gear
Dry clean uniforms
Wool winter class A uniforms
Polyester uniforms - looked great but they're flammable. If you smoked, you know that. Tuned pink if washed with laundry soap
Leather uniform jackets
Car coats were part of winter uniform
John from John's Uniforms traveled the state measuring officers for uniforms
First aid patches on uniform sleeves
Black lanyards
Sam Browne belt
Crupper strap
Round shoulder patch
Shield shoulder patch
Old style bus driver hats, one winter and one summer
Montana Peak hats - don't let Col Mildebrandt see you without it
Male dispatchers wore the highway patrol uniform with a
black and gold "Communication" patch on the right breast
Female employees wore a uniform of consisting of a white blouse and brown skirt.
Gold jackets worn by training staff in the AEOAC road show
Two channel radios
Single small red light in center of patrol car roof
Bubble gum tops mounts

Wooden box to hold all paperwork, made to fit on front seat next to driver
Metal box in trunk to hold equipment, ie. first aid kit, blanket, tow strap, jumper cables, orange pylons, snow tire chains.
fuel transfer device for assisting out off gas motorists
Patrolman Rich Richardson says he carried an umbrella and a portable "potty chair"
Whip antennas
Car to car traffic was signed off with KA2542
Outside full sun visors on patrol cars
Siren switch located on the floorboard next to the dimmer switch. This at times caused embarrassing situations.
Siren located on steering wheel horn ring
Speakers from a drive in theater wired into the patrol vehicle so patrolman could have an outside speaker
Rambler patrol cars
Matador patrol cars
Different colored fully marked patrol cars
Cages in patrol cars
Twin style truck turn signals for top mounts, alternating
one red and one yellow
Moto Guzzi patrol motorcycles
Dispatch centers in Kingman, Flagstaff, Holbrook, Yuma, Phoenix, Claypool, Tucson, and Nogales
Dispatchers used HP or CI before badge numbers to signify uniformed officers or CI units

Dispatchers verbally identifying tower call signs every 30 minutes
Dispatchers in outlying areas had to call Phoenix communications to run a wanted check. That information was kept on cards in a rotating file.
Auto Status
NLETS ticker tapes
Indoor range - Located in present day gym
Transportation was located on the compound, then the Pepsi plant south of McDowell on I-17 and finally at 16th Street
District Five was in a small trailer on the west side of the compound by the training division building
FOCUS, the department's monthly video program
Slightly Out Of Focus, a light hearted, humorous segment at the end of each FOCUS program
DIGEST, the department's monthly newsletter
Paper seal on shotguns to be broken only for official emergency use. Inspected by your sergeant on a monthly basis when he inspected your patrol car.

And now, more stories.

The Taco Squad

Heber John Davis #156

In Nogales, our squad called ourselves the Taco Squad and we were making so many drug arrests, mostly marijuana, that we had to use an old jail cell to store the evidence in. We also seized numerous load vehicles. Some of the vehicles were used by the department for undercover work. Word came down that the cartels were going to put bombs in some of the marijuana bricks and that they had a bounty on me, trying to scare us. I was instructed to call Phoenix headquarters when we made a bust and they would send someone down to X-ray the drugs. We did that a few times, but it was taking so much time that it was unpractical. I decided we would carefully inspect the drugs as we unloaded them. Early one morning Gordon Hopke #403 stopped a big load and he and George Rider #146 took the load vehicle to the Nogales office. As I was carefully inspecting each brick to unload them, an M-80 firecracker exploded under the car. They wanted to see how high the sergeant could jump!

Shots Fired?

Louie Chaboya #1139

George Rider #135 was quite a character/prankster when I worked with him and the rest of the Taco Squad in Nogales. (May he Rest in Peace).

I was training in Nogales in 1973 and was riding with George about 11:00 pm. He got on the frontage road approaching Pala Parado Overpass when he turned off his lights. He told me to be quiet, and we drove on top of the overpass, and he stopped. He then got out and lit two cherry bombs and dropped them onto the median. Why, because he knew that Rudy Acevedo #262 (May he also Rest in Peace) would be snoozing under the overpass. The cherry bombs went off. You can imagine how Rudy felt. He jumped out of his patrol car with his gun drawn looked around and after not seeing anything he got back into his patrol car and headed south towards Nogales. George and I also headed south and later heard that Rudy called in to advise that he was taking a break at Sambos. George also headed to Sambos, and we went in to sit with Rudy. The conversation soon came up when Rudy told us what had happened. He said that maybe he was dreaming but the shots were loud. George did not confess to having dropped the cherry bombs and I also remained quiet.

Two Fer One

John Fink #683

While patrolling I-10 in Tucson near Miracle Mile one night I spotted a vehicle badly weaving in and out of their lane. Thinking for sure the driver was drunk I pulled the vehicle over. I could see there were two occupants - both in the front seat.

I started to get out of my vehicle when I observed a lot of movement between the two occupants. Much to my amazement they were switching seats between the passenger and driver, very slowly and clumsily. I sat back down in my vehicle and waited for the switch to be completed.

I called for another unit to come to my location. Upon approaching the vehicle I asked the 'new ' driver for his license. I then asked the passenger for his license and had him exit the vehicle. I told the 'driver 'to sit tight. While running the 'passenger 'through his paces for being drunk, my backup arrived, and I explained the situation and had him approach the driver. He had the new 'driver 'exit the vehicle also.

Much to our surprise we found that both occupants were drunk out of their minds and ended up arresting the 'passenger 'for driving under the influence of alcohol and the new 'driver 'for being under the influence of alcohol while being in physical control of a motor vehicle.

The Phantom Jack Rabbit

Dick Lewis #176

I was called out one morning about 0200 to go to an accident at the Bylas Bridge on US70.

When I arrived, I found that a westbound vehicle had run off the road on the right at the end of a long sweeping left curve at the end of the bridge. No one was injured.

The driver told me that he dodged around a jack rabbit that was sitting in the road. Actually there were a lot of rabbits there at that time of year! He told me that he had gotten off shift at Morenci at midnight and was headed to Mesa for his days off. It was obvious to me that he had gone to sleep and run off the road.

I wrote him a ticket. He was to answer to the J.P. at Geronimo on a certain date. I called the wrecker from Geronimo to take care of the vehicle.

The wrecker arrived and was pulling the vehicle back onto the road. The driver asked me how much the ticket was going to cost. I said, "I don't know, go ask the wrecker driver, he is the judge!"

He walked up and talked to the judge. The judge (wrecker driver) came back to me and asked how the accident had occurred. I told him what the driver told me and said that I didn't think he went to sleep, and that a two-bit rabbit wasn't worth running off the road for.

The judge said, "Jingo, I don't either. Them rabbits are eating up my garden at home. I'm going to charge him $15.00." Justice was done!

Movie Stars I Have Stopped

Ron Bruce #2048

I happened to make a traffic stop on a VW "Bus" (if you can imagine that) on Interstate 8 eastbound, near the I-10 junction, late one summer evening in the late 1970's or early 1980's. The speed was 67 in the 55 mph nationally mandated limit. On contacting that driver, I found that it was movie/TV actor Robert Blake.

In my career, I never made a big deal when I contacted well known people. I did my introduction and got his California driver's license and vehicle registration. In those days, we were still largely removing the drivers from their vehicles and walking them back to the right front quarter panel area of the cruisers. I explained to Mr. Blake the reason for the stop.

At this point, Blake made it plainly known he did not like police officers and that he thought I was a #@*&. Ignoring him and refusing to be baited into a roadside argument, I wrote the citation and then explained to Blake that his signature was his bond and he could then be on his way. At that time, all traffic violations were still criminal. Blake said I could stick the ticket up my butt, that he was not going to sign it. I reiterated that his signature was mandatory and that it did not indicate any guilt on his part. I also added that if he continued to refuse to sign it, I would have no other option than to arrest him, book him into the local jail and tow his vehicle.

Blake now said I was going to have to fight him before he would consent to an arrest. I calmly flipped the clipboard with the attached citation through the open right front cruiser window and said, “Okay Mr. Blake, if that’s your decision, let’s see what you’ve got.” There was that pregnant pause and Blake responded, “Are you kidding me, you’re actually willing to fight me?” I assure him I was and it was his decision to make. He said, “Fine!!! Give it to me and I’ll sign.” After he did and as I was giving him his copy, I said, “Just what I thought Mr. Blake, alligator mouth and parakeet ass.” I had never cared for the guy anyway. I sent him on his way, and I was grateful that he never filed a complaint.

Working traffic on US 89 north of Flagstaff and south of Gray Mountain, I happened to stop a northbound station-wagon for 67 mph in the 55 mph zone. By now making right side approaches, I contacted the vehicle occupants of which there were four. I thought I recognized the driver and on receipt of his California driver’s license, realized that he was Martin Milner of TV’s “Adam-12” and “Route 66” fame. Milner had a long history in film and television. I brought Milner back to the right front of the cruiser (at that time I was driving one of the six Chevrolet Camaro's that Chevy had given to DPS).

I explained the stop to Milner and he was quite gracious in his responses. I opted to drop the speed to 65+ on the citation, keeping it off of Milner's driving record and explained that to him. He said, he and his buddies were on the way to Lee's Ferry on the Colorado River for some trout fishing. He thanked me for the speed reduction and I sent them on their way. Some days later, when I was at the Flagstaff District Two office, I was telling several of the older Troopers that I had cited Milner. I caught no end of grief for giving a ticket to "Adam-12"!

Working traffic on Interstate 10 another summer evening, I crossed the median near the I-8/I-10 junction, to stop a vehicle with a headlamp out. The car I stopped was a 1957 big-finned Plymouth convertible and Lee Marvin turned out to be the driver. He had a good-looking blonde in the front seat with him, that I assumed was his wife. He never introduced her. After providing his requested paperwork, I explained the reason for the stop. Marvin asked if he could get out and take a look and I said sure. We both walked to the front of the car and found both headlamps working. I asked Marvin to engage the headlamp dimmer switch, which was on the floorboard. He did and both headlamps continued to work. It became obvious I had stopped the wrong vehicle. I assured Marvin that I had no way of knowing that he was the driver from the other side of the interstate, at night and while we were both in motion.

Marvin gave his famous smile and laughed it off and said no problem. We then visited on the side of the highway for close to 15 minutes as I recall. In the end he said they were headed to their home in the Tucson Foothills. He said they had a large place and big swimming pool. He invited me and my family to come down and spend a weekend, that we could drink some whiskey and smoke some cigars and tell each other fabulous lies. I thanked him for his kindness but in the end, never took him up on the offer. Really wish that I had.

Over the 28+ years I spent as a Trooper with the Highway Patrol (3+ as a Reserve in Casa Grande and 25+ as a paid full time Trooper in Casa Grande, Houck and Gray Mountain), I stopped a lot more "famous" people but these are some that really resonated with me.

A Small Town Hero

Bob Singer 2693

I believe it was in the early fall of 1988 when I was stationed in Springerville. I was working the evening shift and met up with a friend of mine who was a captain with the Eagar PD. He told me that Mark Gastineau, the New York Jets MVP and his fiancé Brigitte Nielson, the movie star were in town. That was pretty big news in the little communities of Springerville and Eager. Mark grew up in Eagar, played football for Round Valley High School and his mother owned a bed and breakfast there. Mark would come up every now and then to visit his mother.

Mark had bought a brand new Ford F250 four door 4X4 truck and he and Brigitte were driving it around town. I told him I knew they were in town and had seen the two of them in the truck. The captain told me that Mark had an outstanding warrant for his arrest. I asked him if they were going to arrest him and he said "no, he is our small town hero." I told him that we were sworn to uphold the law and that if he wouldn't do it, I would. After a few more minutes of talking, I went to our little "103", a small single wide trailer on the east edge of town and called Flagstaff dispatch. I did that because I knew that everyone in the two small towns had scanners and would hear it. I didn't want to give what I was going to do away. All I knew was his name, so I had her run a driver's license check and an ACIC/NCIC check. Within a few seconds she said she had a sound alike matching his description with a suspended New York driver's license and an MCSO misdemeanor warrant for failing to show a water skier down flag. Apparently he was the driver of the boat pulling a water skier who went down in the water and Mark didn't lift up a water skier down flag so MCSO lake patrol cited him. His New York driver's license was also suspended in Arizona for not paying a civil fine on a traffic ticket. I told her that he was in town now at the Safari restaurant and I would wait to talk to him when he came out. I remember her telling me that "he is a pretty big buff guy so I'll get backup when you tell me you're stopping him."

With the warrant and suspension information in hand, I found the truck still parked at the restaurant. I pulled into a parking lot across the street and turned my lights off and waited. Within a few minutes, Mark, Brigitte and another man and woman came out of the restaurant and got into the big Ford truck and pulled out of the parking lot with Mark driving onto main street in Springerville. I notified dispatch that I was going to pull over Mark and I turned on my headlights, pulled onto the street behind his truck and turned on all of my lights. The truck turned right and pulled over immediately on a side street with me stopping behind it. I walked up to the truck and asked the driver, Mark, to step out with his driver's license and had him walk back to the right side of my patrol car. I didn't want to embarrass him in front of the other people in the car. When we got to the right side of my patrol car, I told him that I had stopped him because of the outstanding warrant and driving while suspended in Arizona. I also called dispatch and told her that I was code 4 and didn't need a backup. He told me that his agent was supposed to have taken care of that and didn't know about the unpaid traffic ticket.

About this time, Brigitte got out of the front passenger side of the truck and walked back. I remember she had on a mink stole that wrapped around her neck and shoulders, tight pants and knee high black boots. She asked what was going on and Mark told her. She started crying and talking about all of the problems they had had lately and her medical problems at which time he told her to go back and get in the truck. All of this had been in a very calm manner. After she got in the truck, the male back seat passenger got out and walked back. He asked what was going on and Mark told him. He was standing in front of me and just to the right at a safe distance. I had already told Mark what the bond was on the warrant which he said he didn't have in his wallet. I told the passenger what the bond was and that he was going to have to go to the Apache County jail and post it or be booked into jail. The man put his hand into his front pocket and pulled out a big roll of bills and said "what is it going to take to make this go away?" I told him what the bond amount was again and he said "Look, I was a Chicago police officer once and know how this works. How much will it take?" as he started peeling off twenty-dollar bills. I told him that he better put that back in his pocket and get back in the truck or he would be going to jail with Mark for trying to bribe a police officer. He quickly turned and got back in the truck. I told Mark that I had never tried this before but since it was only about 6pm, I would have my dispatcher call the court clerk and see if she would come out to the courthouse and take his bond since the passenger had enough to pay it. A minute later, dispatch called me back and said the court clerk would be right out. I had dispatch run the passengers driver's license and check ACIC and NCIC which came back good. I asked Mark if the passenger could drive them over to the courthouse to wait for the court clerk which he agreed to so we drove around the block to the courthouse parking lot.

After parking, I got out an arrest form from my trunk, sat down in my driver's seat and started filling it out to save time. I got about half way done when Mark got out of his truck and walked over to the passenger side of my car. I motioned for him to open the door and when he did, he sheepishly said, "can I sit in here with you? There is too much drama going on in the truck." I let him sit down with his feet outside the car while we waited. After a few minutes, Sherri, the court clerk showed up and had two teenage girls with her. One was her daughter, and the other was her daughter's best friend. When we all got inside the court, the passenger posted the bond, and all was done. As we started to walk back out of the court, Sherri asked Mark if he would sign the two girls autograph books for them that they brought with them. He laughed and signed them. Another day in the life of a small-town Highway Patrol Officer.

Why The Gloves?

Larry Scarber #3954

I don't recommend holding an owl, but this story had a happy ending. From late 1987 to early 1991, I was a rookie Highway Patrolman living in Kayenta. Late one evening, I saw what I thought was a large rock on the highway west of Kayenta. There were ore hauling trucks passing along US 160 at the time, and they occasionally spilled part of their load. This one looked big enough to do a lot of damage to a vehicle. I stopped to remove it and discovered it was an owl, an adult Great Horned owl, to be more precise. I tried shooing it from the road, but it wouldn't budge. Using my baton, I pushed it from the traffic lane. It would fall over and then pop back up.

I called my dispatcher, and they called Game & Fish. I was asked to check the owl's pupils. They were dilated and didn't respond to light, and the iris of one eye appeared to be torn. I was told that it probably flew into the side of a truck. I could leave it there for the coyotes or take it home, but it would likely die during the night. I was cautioned that if it died, I should bury it and not keep any feathers, as they were illegal to possess. If it should survive the night, I was to call Game & Fish the next day to arrange a pick-up.

I put the owl on the passenger side floor of my patrol car and drove home. It was late, but Jeannie and I awakened our three young children (Bill, Joe, and Katie) so they could see and pet the owl.

The following day the owl was still alive. I prepared for work, and Jeannie took a video of me holding the owl. I drove toward Kaibeto with the owl in an open box on the front seat. A Game & Fish ranger from Page met me along the highway. We met between our cars, and he asked where the owl was? I told him it was on the front seat. He returned to his truck and donned a pair of heavy gloves that nearly reached his elbows. I asked what they were for? He explained that if the owl sunk its talons into an arm, it would require pliers to remove them. I thought that would have been a handy bit of information the previous night before I placed the owl in my car and had my kids wake up to see our honored guest.

The ranger explained that the owl would be taken to the Adobe Mountain Rehab facility in Phoenix. I thought that would be my last time seeing the owl.

Months later, I was in Phoenix to work security at the Arizona State Fair. While wandering around the fairgrounds, I stopped by the Arizona Game & Fish booth and saw what I thought was a stuffed owl...until it moved its head. I asked the ranger at the booth about the owl. He said it was blind and so docile that they would take it to schools for demonstrations. I asked if he knew where it came from, and he said it had been at Adobe Mountain until a few months ago and before that had been rescued from the Navajo Reservation. I was able to fill him in on the details.

I'm glad Jeannie took the video, or no one would believe this story.

Can I Borrow Some Panty Hose

Bob Ticer #4490

One night back in the 90's I was patrolling State Route 69 out of the Prescott Office looking for drunk drivers. The night was slow, and I just couldn't find any drunks on the highway so I drove into Prescott Valley to see if I could "poach" a local. It didn't take me long until I found a drunk driver, who I stopped in a local neighborhood. The driver, a young female, was not too pleasant to deal with. After placing her in the back seat of my patrol car, I sat back in the vehicle to complete some paperwork when I heard a guttural noise and then felt something wet hit the back of my neck. Yes, it was spit from the driver. Well, I wasn't too happy about that so I stepped out to cool down and went to my trunk to see if I could find something to put over her head before transport. Of course, I had nothing, and this was before spit masks were a commonly issued item.

About this time, a nice elderly woman stepped out of the house across the street and asked if I needed any help. Remembering that I heard sometime in the past that panty hose was a good option to stop spitters if you put the stocking over the person's head, like a bank robber. I asked the elderly woman if she had an old pair of panty hose that I could borrow and put over my driver's head because she had spat on me. The nice lady said, "I'll be right back." When she returned, she said, "Officer, I only have this new pair of Leggs, but you can have them, and she shouldn't spit on you." I said thank you and told the lady that I would return them. She said, "It's okay, keep them." After applying the "spit mask", I transported the driver to the Yavapai County Jail. I am sure that some folks that night thought this patrolman had a bank robber in custody.

One Way To Make Your Point

Frank Glenn #468

It was back in the middle 70's I was issued a crew cab truck with a service bed on it. At that time, I only had one place on the compound to park that monster. I am sure it is all different now but it was at the top of the stairs leading down to the old armory, and indoor range. The command staff along with their admin sergeants were all in a building just to the west of the stairs.

I had been gone for a period of time one day and when I came back there was a car parked in my spot. What the heck! Well, I parked in front of that car blocking it in and went on down to the armory. Not too long after that Major Snedigar's admin sergeant Rick Ayers came down to the armory and started shooting the bull about this and that. I was wondering why he might be there as he had never been in to armory before. Soon enough he asks if that truck belonged to one of us which I thought was rather surprising as I had been parking that truck there for two years. I said yes that is my truck and then he said "you are going to have to move it because you are blocking the major." I replied well, I leave at 1700. Rick said man, I cannot tell him that! I said if you don't who is going to tell him.

Rick left and I fully expected to be standing tall in front of the major's desk just any moment. Nothing happens the rest of the day so I head out to leave at 1700, get in to my truck crank it over and it will not start. Three of the other admin sergeants were standing outside smirking. I got out and looked under the hood and not only was my coil wire unplugged it was gone. Ok, I walk into where the major was and he is sitting at his desk talking on the phone looking at a clock on the wall and he never looked at me but I know he knows I am there and I leave and go outside. Right at 1730 out he comes, we howdy each other and pretty soon he pulled my coil wire out of this pocket and said “is this yours”? I replied I was not sure but thought I could make it work. He handed it to me and said the reason I was parked there is because someone else parked in my spot. He said should you find me there in the future would you leave the keys in the truck so I can move to if I need to go somewhere. I replied yes sir I can do that. Figuring I had pushed this as far as I should I didn’t ask him why he didn’t block that person.

The major made his point and nobody’s feathers got ruffled. To this day I have great respect for him and several I could name should have taken lessons from him.

Just Wondering

Paul Palmer #342

On April 4, 1968, I was dispatching in Holbrook. That night a teletype came across advising of the assassination of Martin Luther King in Memphis, Tennessee. The APB stated a vehicle in connection with the crime was a white Mustang.

I broadcast the APB but within hours another APB from the FBI came through advising to disregard the information on the white Mustang. Without much thought, I broadcast this information. I put the information out of my mind

but for some reason over the years I have never forgotten the cancellation APB on the Mustang.
Over the years I have read books about the assassination and learned that the white Mustang was located in Atlanta, Georgia days after the assassination.
If the Mustang wasn't located until days later, why the APB to disregard the information on the Mustang so soon after the murder?
I'm not a conspiracy nut, but is it a coincidence that an APB from the FBI was issued relating to a white Mustang, followed by cancellation of the wanted Mustang, then followed by the Mustang being located days later?
Just wondering.

The Little Violators

Dick Lewis #176

One summer afternoon I was patrolling west of Miami, approaching the Castle Dome mine road. I found myself behind a sedan with a woman driver. The car was two seated and there were two boys about seven or eight jumping around and generally annoying the driver. I could see that she was annoyed and was trying to make them behave.
This was before we generally had air conditioning in our cars, and our windows were down. So I turned on my lights and the car pulled over in a wide spot. As I walked up to the car on the left side, I said in a very loud voice, "Which one of

these boys do you want me to take to jail?" The woman picked up on it and replied, "Take them both!" So I lectured the boys on how important it was to behave and not distract the driver.
It was a friendly contact and as she drove away the kids were seated correctly with their hands folded in their laps. They were looking straight ahead. I bet they were good all the way home!

The Tyson Gang

Heber John Davis #156

While I was stationed in Tucson, the Tyson gang broke out of the state prison and went on a killing rampage across several states, prompting the largest manhunt in Arizona history. With the city, county and Indian police we placed roadblocks in several locations in District 8. We had an emergency response plan in place to call out officers to man the roadblocks. We wanted to prevent them from going to Mexico. Early one morning I received a call about a possible sighting of the gang, so we put a plan in place to man the roadblocks.. At one of the roadblocks they tried to run the block by firing at the officers. The officers returned fire, killing the driver and their killing rampage ended. The movie "Killer in the family" starring Robert Mitchum was based on the Tyson gang.

The Tyson Gang Prison Break

Dennis McNulty #1959

I was hired by DPS in November 1976 as a dispatcher in Phoenix op-comm. On July 30th, 1978, Gary Tyson's three sons staged an armed prison escape from the visitors area at the state prison in Florence where they broke out their father, Gary Tyson, and another inmate by the name of Randy Greenwalt. Tyson was serving life for murder and Greenwalt was a convicted serial killer. They all then engaged in a three-state crime spree that resulted in six murders.

Thursday August 10th 1978 I was on a day off. Every second Thursday was payday at DPS and, dressed in shorts, T-shirt and flip-flops, I drove to op-comm to get my check. In those days you had to get your paper pay check at work and then deposit it. It was in the early evening and as I was chatting with co-workers, word came out that someone attempted a break in at the Border Patrol station in Gila Bend. There was an ongoing statewide manhunt for the Tyson Gang and they were suspected in being involved in the break in.

The on-duty op-comm supervisor, Patty Crum #1008 grabbed me and said she was shorthanded and that I was now on duty with overtime. I was put on the district 4 radio console so she could isolate each district with a designated dispatcher.

Early on the morning of August 11th, the Tyson Gang left Casa Grande in a stolen van heading east on Chuichu highway. They crashed through a roadblock set up by the Pinal County Sheriff's Office and continued to flee at high speed east on Chuichu highway when they came upon a second Pinal County roadblock. Deputies at this roadblock opened fire with rifles. One of Tyson's sons was driving, and he was hit and killed by gunfire, causing the van to crash.

The deputies from the second roadblock along with pursuing deputies from the first roadblock took the other two Tyson sons and Randy Greenwalt into custody. At some point Gary Tyson was able to escape on foot and flee onto the desert.

At Phoenix op-comm we were getting this real time through a hook up with Pinal County SO op-comm in Florence. We also had DPS command level officers with us in op-comm to coordinate DPS road units in district 6 (Casa Grande and Pinal County). They were cheering on the report of the shootout.

On August 22nd 1978 I was on day shift in op-comm working the phones. The statewide manhunt operation under the command of the Coconino County Sheriff had moved their command post to the training building on the DPS compound. In the early afternoon I answered a phone call from a guy who worked at the chemical plant near the Chuichu highway. He was calling to say he had followed a bad smell at the rear of the plant where he could see the decomposing body of a large man beneath an ironwoods tree. I switched his call to the command post.

Responding officers found that it was Gary Tyson's body and evidence showed he had died hard from heat exposure and no water. A .45 caliber Colt pistol was found under his body.

Hey, There's A Parade Coming!

Dick Lewis #176

Sometime back I was working the Payson Rodeo Parade. The famous August doins', first rodeo ever.

I had to for some reason, re-route the parade a couple of blocks off its usual route to come out on Main Street next to the Sheriff's office. I had the traffic re-routed so as to not get in the way of the parade.

Here came a U.S. Postal Service jeep mail man up the wrong way into the route. The parade hadn't shown up yet. I stopped the vehicle and told the driver that he couldn't go up that way. He said, "You cannot stop me, I'm the U.S. mail and I can go. You can't tell me where I can go." He was very insolent about it so I said, "OK, go ahead," and he went.

In less than two minutes he returned. As he passed by headed in the other way, he slowed and said in a shout, "Hey, there's a parade coming down there.

What a fool!

A City of Phoenix Bus Has The Right Of Way

Colin Peabody #481

One afternoon in about 1980, the Phoenix PD was investigating a fatal accident at 23rd Ave and Indian School Road about 300 yards east of the I-17 interchange at Indian School. This is a three way intersection and there were no north or south side streets between the freeway interchange and 23rd Ave. The PD requested that we divert all eastbound traffic on Indian School and all northbound frontage road traffic to go north on the frontage from Indian School. The PD had all southbound traffic blocked for 23rd. Ave. Motor Officer Steve Mason #408 drew the duty of diverting that traffic and was doing a great job of getting the traffic to do what was necessary until an eastbound City of Phoenix bus pulled up and started through the intersection toward the accident scene. Steve stopped the bus and the driver was adamant that his route required him to go through there and he was not going to divert. The bus was full of passengers and it was obvious to them of the emergency traffic directly ahead of them a couple hundred yards, with police and fire vehicles blocking the roadway. Steve came on board the bus and patiently explained the reason the bus had to divert. The bus driver became more demanding that he was going ahead because of the length and wheelbase of the bus, he couldn't make the turn onto the northbound frontage. His bus was now parked in the center lane of eastbound Indian School Road. As Steve's sergeant, I was called to the scene and we still couldn't reason with the driver, with him maintaining his bus couldn't make that turn. We called the bus company and told them the problem and what the bus driver was refusing to do in obeying lawful orders. During this time the driver became unruly and was advised he was going to be cited for failure to obey a lawful order and we were going to tow the bus. We advised the bus company of that as well. They called their driver and advised him to follow our orders, which he did in a little while. In the meantime, we secured witness statements from all of the passengers in the front rows of the bus, and each of them verified the actions of the bus driver and how Officer Mason and I were handling the situation. The driver was subsequently cited and he did move the bus.

A day later, we were advised that the City of Phoenix Transit had filed a complaint against us because we wouldn't allow their bus driver to proceed as we had directed and that our officers, (Steve Mason and me), had made the bus travel in a movement that was too tight for it to maneuver in safety. I called the Transit outfit and gave them the bus number and asked them to provide me with the physical dimensions of that bus, length, width, wheelbase and turning radius, which they did. We drew a diagram of the intersection on top at Indian School and exactly where the bus was placed, and the route the bus would have taken to get on the northbound frontage by following our order to do so.

Once we had enough information we met with officials at the bus company at their lot off Durango and 27th Ave. The bus in question was present as was the driver. We presented our investigative information, which also included information from Phoenix PD about the fatal accident covering the entire intersection of 23rd Ave, preventing any traffic from getting through, as well as all our witness statements from the occupants of the bus. Apparently, the bus driver hadn't fully told his supervisors the information about where his bus was sitting while all this was going on. You could have put two busses identical to the one in question into a turn on the frontage road and both would have been able to make the turn without interfering with the other unit. Once they saw our "evidence", the driver became unemployed on the spot and apologies were made by the Transit Officials to both Officer Mason, myself and to the DPS for the actions of their driver. The complaint was resolved to everyone's satisfaction but the driver. He was still stuck with the ticket as a lesson the City of Phoenix busses don't always have the right of way.

Governor Jack Williams

Heber John Davis #156

In 1967 Patrolman Jim Gallery was working an extra job unloading tires from a railroad car in Phoenix. I was working with him and we were putting the tires in a warehouse, a very dirty job, when Patrolman Don Gump came in. Don and I worked Grand Avenue together and I had told him where I would be on my days off. He said "Davis, get your ass down to my patrol car, they want you to interview you for the Governor's Security Job. " He took me home so I could get cleaned up and go to the interview, I got the job and worked with Sgt. Neil McLeod and Ptlm George Rider until 1969 when I was sent to Nogales as a newly promoted Sergeant. In 1973, I was sent back to Phoenix to supervise Executive Security near the end of Governor Jack Williams term. Governor Williams told me the thing he would miss the most was the magnificent men of the Highway Patrol when he left office. What a wonderful compliment for the Department.

That Time I Stole a Dog, and Missed a Funeral

A. Whitney 1410

Of all the people I met while an Arizona Highway Patrolman, one I remember with a whole lot of fondness is Officer Gene Fredricks. He was 1389, I was 1410. We were classmates in the academy,

and when we graduated were both assigned to Winslow. After a couple of months, when the district boundaries changed, we were both transferred to the Flagstaff District, but along with Don Williams, stayed in Winslow.
Gene and I both had, um, *unusual* senses of humor…
Gene seemed to just love finding my Ray-Bans on the squad room table and pick them up, depositing as many finger and thumb smears on the lenses as he could. He might also comment on how shiny my badge was and do the same thing, except he left the badge pinned to my shirt…
Now, if you recall, the early '70's brought the dreaded ***"Gas Crisis!!"*** Suddenly, the freeways were empty, and we patrolmen were restricted in our mileage. About 80 miles per shift, as I recall. Gene and I were most off-put by the situation, and combining our somewhat nefarious thinkers, came up with a plan. There was this stretch of frontage road north of I-40 that ran from MP 245, Leupp Road, East to… nowhere. (Actually, it served as an access to the Turquoise Ranch, but nobody lived there.)
So. We noticed that in reverse, the old mechanical odometers would subtract miles…
A bit later in the crisis, Gene and I were assigned to patrol in one car. The mileage restriction remained. We were very safe, but bored. We wished that we'd had a radar, a VASCAR, or *sumpin'*… One of us noticed my Thermos bottle. It

was a big one, and was sort of mustard colored, with a beige bottom. If you held it just right and pointed it out the window, it looked a lot like a radar unit…

Thus was born the fabled "TR-1410" of song and legend!

Remember what I said about the smudges on my specs and badge? Well one day, I resolved to get even. As Gene pulled up to the gas pumps in the Winslow ADOT yard, I waited; a moderately large, and very dusty rock behind my back. As smiling Gene came to a stop, through the open driver's window I deposited said rock to the lap of the now smile-less squad mate.

I think he forgave me in a month or so…

But the dangdest thing I saw from Gene took place in Happy Jack. Our Sergeant Pat Lee, 161, had inveigled the use of a Forest Service barracks for an over-night squad meeting. One of the Flagstaff members of our squad was Rick Eimerman. (Did I mention that whisky and beer were freely available, and freely partaken? Well they were, and were most *certainly* freely partaken!)

Now, there came a point where Rick, who by the way wore horn rim eyeglasses, felt the need to become supine on one of the bunks. For some reason, he forgot to remove his glasses. Perhaps all that Bourbon had confused the poor boy.

At any rate, there came Gene, holding an aerosol of shaving cream. He gently placed a thick coat of the suds on the lenses of the glasses on the face of

the unfortunate Rick, who awoke screaming that he had gone blind.
(What *was* this fascination Gene had for glasses, anyhow?)
Then, almost six years ago, came the sad news that Gene had had a stroke. I went to Flagstaff to see him. Although Gene was not conscious, I spoke to him. I hope he heard me…
Shortly after, Gene died.
The wake was in Winslow. The funeral was set for the next morning, in Kykotsmovi. (Gene was a Hopi.)
Now the only motel in the area was at the Hopi Cultural Center, so I reserved a room.
As I parked in the lot, I was greeted by this little dark brown dog, with amazing golden eyes. She jumped up on me, and I spent a little time with her.
Next morning after breakfast, I walked to where I had parked, hoping that the dog wasn't still hanging around.
She was asleep under *my* car!
DAMN!
I happen to be a very mean man, as many of you doubtless know. But I ain't *that* mean!
"Do you want to come live with me in Prescott?"
"Yeth, misther."
So I was on the horns of a dilemma. Headed for Gene's service, unexpected dog in tow, no collar, no leash. I did the only thing I could think of.
Went to the church, explained the problem, and excused myself. I don't think Gene minded…

As for the dog? Her name is Ma No, which I am told is "Little Girl" in the Hopi language.
All through the journey home, she vomited clear liquid. There was no food in there... She puked on the seats. On the floor. In my open suitcase. But mostly, she vomited on me!
OhGodwhathaveIdone????? I've stolen a dog with PARVO! Or maybe DISTEMPER! RABIES!!!!!
IT'S GOTTA BE RABIES!!!!
A stop at the veterinarian got the diagnosis that she was just plain old car sick. Also, it yielded a bag of dog food. (The dog I already had was on a prescription diet.) We got home, the bag was opened, and little Ma No (who now weighs about 50 pounds) disappeared head-first into it!
So that's my story of how I stole a dog and missed a funeral. Ma No is doing very well; as the sole female in the house, she rules with an iron paw.
I'm not saying that Doggie Blue or Dooley the Dog are *afraid* of her, exactly, but she sure gets a whole lot of respect…
Now my foundling has a home. She sleeps on the bed, curled up with her back pressed against mine. But I still can't take her no place in no car…

A Very Stupid Hunter

Dennis McNulty #1959

In 1983, a new patrolman was assigned to Dist. 3 (name lost to the mist of time) and he was being shown the District. I was assigned to show him around Winslow. Since we would sometimes make violator stops east of Winslow in Coconino County (the Winslow City limits was the Navajo/Coconino county line, we were driving over to Flagstaff so I could show him where the Flag JP court and the county jail were and some of the better code-7 locations. Near the exit for Two Guns (which had an old KOA camp ground and an abandoned gas station), I-40 sort of curves south and crosses over the Devil's Canyon bridge. In this area, south of the interstate, you could sometimes see herds of prong horned antelope on the treeless prairie. As we approached this area, we see a pickup truck stopped in the medium. Thinking we had a code-34, I started to pull into the medium to render aid. The PU driver, who was standing outside the vehicle obviously didn't see or hear us because he reached into the PU cab and pulled out what we later found to be a scoped Remington .308 hunting rifle which he proceeded to put to his shoulder and point at passing E/B traffic. We let out a collective "Oh shit". I slammed on the brakes and we both exited my car with drawn guns. The surprised driver fortunately obeyed our commands to lay the rifle on the ground and put his hands up. Our questioning of this knucklehead revealed that he was a resident of Flagstaff and he had been drawn by Game & Fish to hunt pronghorns. He knew about the herds south of the interstate and he was just there using his scope to check them out. We explained to this idiot that pointing a rifle across passing traffic just might upset some folks and could he stop being a stupid SOB and go spot wildlife elsewhere. We swapped autographs with him on a citation for illegal parking on the highway and sent him packing. You get to meet all kinds on the interstate.

The Bar Fight

John Fink, #683

Back in the early 70's I spotted a vehicle weaving eastbound on Benson Highway in Tucson. I wasn't sure if the driver was drunk as it was still late afternoon. As I tried to pull the vehicle over it made a left turn into the parking lot of the Rainbow Tavern. I approached the driver, and he did in fact seem to be under the influence. He exited the vehicle and as I was running him through the paces a group of patrons from the bar came out into the parking lot and began harassing me and was telling the driver of the vehicle to quit cooperating in the field sobriety test. There was one individual who was the ring leader of the group. I tried to ignore the group and called for a backup while trying to get the driver to cooperate. My backup, Warren Cottrell, arrived just as the crowd was getting extremely hostile. I placed the drunk driver under arrest, cuffed him and put him in my vehicle. The ring leader of the crowd continued to try to interfere and I asked him to come to me, that I wanted to talk to him. He stated loudly that if I wanted him I would have to come inside to get him and with that he went back into the bar. Warren asked me if I wanted him and I said yes as I was going to arrest him for interference. Warren said let's go get him.

As we both entered the bar it took a minute for our eyes to adjust. The individual I wanted was behind the bar and was wiping the bar down. There were other patrons sitting at the bar that were to our left and the opening to go behind the bar was at the far end. I told the individual to step outside as I wanted to 'talk 'to him. He said, "I'm tending bar and get out." We made our way to the far end of the bar to escort the individual out when all of a sudden he pulled a handgun out from under the bar and pointed it at us and again told us to get out. Warren pushed me back and told me to get out. I moved back so that Warren and I were separated by about 10 feet. We both had our hands on our weapons ready to draw. The individual's hand with the weapon was shaking severely as he was pointing the gun first on Warren and then on me, moving it back and forth. We continued to talk to him, telling him to put the weapon down and that we just wanted to talk to him. He finally put the gun down on the bar and stepped back. We headed around the far end of the bar to apprehend the suspect and secure the weapon.

As we were approaching the opening of the bar another individual reached and grabbed the gun. Warren was ahead of me and jumped on the

individual. The bartender joined in as I did and the four of us starting wrestling. Warren was wrestling with the individual with the gun and I was wrestling with the bartender.
I then heard the gun go off and the individual that Warren was wrestling with went down. I had the bartender on the ground and was in the process of handcuffing him. Warren asked if I had this and he went out to his vehicle to call for help.

While handcuffing the bartender someone must have helped the gunshot victim out the back door.
Warren returned and we were getting ready to pick the bartender up off the floor and escort him out to my vehicle.
I had failed to mention that the bar was pretty full and there were numerous patrons sitting at the bar as this situation unfolded. They immediately started to rise and climb over the bar stating that we weren't going to take the bartender anywhere.
At this time our first backup arrived who was Sonny Wimberly. As he came through the door he jacked a round into his shotgun. All of those patrons that were climbing over the bar immediately sat back down.
That round going into the chamber of that shotgun was the most beautiful sound that I have ever heard. After all these years I can still recall what that sounded like.
The scene was secured and we loaded the bartender into a police vehicle. The drunk driver

was still sitting in my vehicle waiting for transport to jail.

The bartender was in his mid-50's and we later learned that the other individual who had escaped with a gunshot wound was his son in his late 20's.

As we were booking both the drunk driver and the bartender we heard that the investigators had completed their search of the bar and could not locate the gun. Our story was starting to be questioned about the gun and it was getting imperative that we locate it.

As we were at the office completing our paperwork we received a call from Tucson Medical Center that a gunshot victim matching our description of the individual from the bar was being treated for a gunshot wound in the emergency room. We immediately headed to TMC and arrested this individual who had received a superficial wound to his abdomen.

After he was booked and after we completed our paperwork Warren and I headed home. We were still puzzled as to the whereabouts of the gun.

It was probably about midnight when I finally was able to fall asleep. About 3 or 4 in the morning my phone rang. It was Warren. He said that he had just gotten out of bed, went out to his car and looked under his front seat and there was the gun. He finally realized while sleeping that he remembered he put it in his vehicle when he went out to call for backup.

A trauma incident can do weird things to one's mind. Thank goodness he finally remembered where the gun was.

After a lengthy trial, both individuals were sent up to Florence.

Back in the early 70's, I was still a rookie. I remember in the Academy that 'Courteous Vigilance 'was drilled into us. That was what I believe I was trying to mimic inside that bar. We were extremely fortunate things turned out the way they did. I definitely would have handled the situation much differently today!

Not In My Area!

Greg Eavenson #680

After 8 or 9 months in Blythe, Keith Neitch 412 moved his family to Parker which left the Ehrenberg state trailer available for my wife and I. Yuma county had moved their Quartzite deputy so I got called by citizens to handle family fights and sometimes bar fights.

The post office shared a common wall with the A-1 bar which was notorious for unruly patrons. I always checked our post office box at the end of each shift and several times I became involved in bar brawls.

One occasion a citizen notified me that there was going to be a "shoot out "next door at the A-1. Inside I met up with a big fella who told me that a guy had been messing with his wife but wouldn't fist fight him. The guy had gone to Blythe to get his gun so he was going to get his also. I looked at his wife and, whew! Flys wouldn't even light on her. I asked the big fella where he lived, and he said "Blythe ". I told him he should go home immediately, get his gun and shoot the other dude first, but do so in "Blythe". Fortunately I never heard of a shoot-out in Blythe after that.

Officer Down?

Louie Chaboya #1139

Charlie Knapp #1260, Harold Swyers #3424 (May he rest in peace) and I were assigned to the narcotic squad in Nogales. There was a case where we received information that a load of marijuana would be heading to Tucson. We were given the description of the vehicle and time. Sure enough the vehicle was spotted northbound on I-19 and Charlie and I in Charlie's vehicle followed the vehicle and stopped it. Charlie went for the driver, and I went for the passenger. The passenger then ran towards the frontage. The side of the road was full of weeds about two to three feet tall. The passenger jumped the right-away fence and started running south. I started running after him but after about half a mile lost and sight of him in all the produce warehouse in the area. I then started walking back to the vehicles to help Charlie. By now Charlie had back up that included Harold and three officers. As I approached the vehicles, I noticed that all 5 were looking through the weeds as if searching for what I thought was the load of marijuana. As I got closer, I asked, "What are you all looking for? 'They all looked up and Charlie said with a few choice words: "You blankaty blankaty blank, we were looking for you!!!, The guy shot at you Louie".

I never heard the shots. The driver was arrested but the passenger got away. Over 100 pounds of marijuana were found in the trunk of the vehicle.

Why I Now "Hablo Un Poco Español"

Steve Gendler #1064

As a newly minted rookie straight out of the academy in the early 1970's I found myself assigned to a veteran squad while living in Toltec and covering the area south of Coolidge, Eloy and Casa Grande. This presented an opportunity to work with some very colorful characters that were eager to add their "real life" knowledge and experience to what I had learned in the academy. These lessons usually occurred during a meal break, or, as the sergeant called it, "swatting flies" while parked car-to-car in the median.

Now take for instance Frank Reyes, my nearest squad member, who lived down the road in Picacho and Leo Smith who worked out of Red Rock. They told me about the time Leo had stopped a car with three illegal aliens and called

Frank to “interpret” since Frank spoke Spanish. Apparently there was a long conversation in Spanish, and the three suspects began looking Leo up and down menacingly. “What the ^%$%$ did you tell them Frank” said Leo, “aw just that if they could take you they were free to go” said Frank.

The Paper Weight

Paul Palmer #342

I had the pleasure of working with Sgt Russ Dunham in the Training Division in the early 80’s. Russ is the nicest guy you ever wanted to meet. He is one of those rare individuals that you never hear anyone say a bad word about.

One Monday morning Russ came to work and over coffee he told us that a traveling circus was crossing the country and had to stop for the night in Wickenburg. They were looking for a place to stop where they could feed, water and bed down their animals. As you can imagine finding a spot for lions, elephants, monkeys and all the other animals that are in a circus was a difficult thing to do. Someone mentioned that Russ Dunham’s mom had a place that would have room for them.

Russ was up at his mom’s place the weekend the circus rolled up to her place. Russ began to tell us about all the animals and said that the elephants had the biggest poop you ever saw. It looks like a pile of straw, and it doesn’t stink he told us.

A light bulb flashed bright in my warped brain. I told Russ to get some elephant poop and spray it with polyurethane and we could use it as paper weights. The next week Russ brought in a box of large polyurethane covered elephant turds. Sure enough they looked like straw and the polyurethane gave them a nice shine. Several of us had them on our desks.

At the time Phoenix Police Sgt Harry Florian taught some kind of class in the training building. Harry Florian was the Phoenix PD PIO and if you remember was a regular on the Wallace and Ladmo show. Harry was a real kick.

One day prior to his going into the classroom to teach his class, he was sitting in my office visiting. It wasn't long before he picked up the elephant paper weight and was examining it. He couldn't stand it any longer and finally asked what it was. I told him we had one for him and then explained what it was. Harry's eyes got big, and he jumped up, hollered and threw my paper weight across the room. When he returned to my office after washing his hands he said that, no, he didn't think he wanted one.

What a shame. It isn't often you are offered a one of a kind item that no one else will ever have.

Some Cadet Humor

T.K. Waddell #803

I thought of the many stories I could write about: the blonde female wearing only a bikini and high heels hitchhiking on I-40; the time a skunk got the best of me towards the end of my shift; or the time I made a traffic stop, and the violator observed that I was not wearing my pistol belt. But, I thought I should poke some fun at myself with this story.

I was in my last week of OJT riding with my future partner Tom Gosch 1172. I was driving his vehicle because it was equipped with VASCAR, a very desired speed tool. Learning VASCAR was something that few were able to experience. As evening fell Tom said he wanted to show me some points of interest on I-40 i.e. hidden median crossovers, good staging points for VASCAR etc. because things looked different at night. He also wanted to see my nighttime high speed driving skills.

Well OK, So we were heading up Ash Fork hill at a reasonable high rate of speed. Ok, maybe not so reasonable. He was saying that at 60mph +, if you see it, you will probably hit it. (headlights were not so good in the early 70's) Well, as luck might have it, as I started to pass a Semi-truck as it lumbered along in the right lane. The semi-truck hit a small deer, vaulting it into my lane. Tom was right, I had just recognized the animal when I hit it. We pulled over and moved the deceased animal off to the side of the road. Tom then proceeded to test my car/deer accident report writing. Following that, he had me demonstrate my 1st aid abilities by splinting and putting bandages on this poor busted up creature. The irony of this is that I had a valid hunting license and deer tag for this area. I didn't get to keep the game.

I passed all his OJT training requirements and returned to Phoenix to finish the remaining weeks of the academy. Never let anything be known to the training staff, if an example could be made of a cadet! I received a special gift from the staff. (Colin Peabody and SGT. Jim Eaves) Since I was one of the vertically challenged officers, upon graduation, I was awarded a booster seat and wooden blocks for the brake and gas pedal, so as to help enable me to see animals or obstructions in the roadway. Ha a, the joke was on me and what a thoughtful gift!

I should have kept those wonderful gifts. Had I known that later in the year, I would be assigned our old district swing car. It was, as many may remember a rolling land yacht. A 1972 429 cubic inch Mercury. It was faster in 3rd gear, than in overdrive. They were too large for two lane roads like SR-89 or US-66. Not enough room to make a U-turn, so they were assigned mainly to the Interstate highways. Well, this old relic had 60+ thousand miles, and worn out shocks. The seat springs were so worn down I could hardly see over the steering wheel. The seat was locked about 3 inches back to accommodate the Motorola radio and a home build flattop console, for writing reports etc. When I drove it, I could imagine other motorists seeing a police car rolling down the road with no visible driver. However, I was there, looking like a 10yr old kid in his dads car playing with the steering wheel.

This old Merc had a trunk the size of a long bed pickup truck. It had a metal box that held a case of flares, a first aid kit the size of a lumberjacks toolbox, a rain poncho, a wool blanket, 1 gallon of water, a tow strap, a shovel and other miscellaneous items. The trunk still had room for two more cases of flares, a universal car jack, a 4 way lug wrench, 10lb fire extinguisher, a spare tire, 5 highway cones and the district radio. All of that and it still had enough room for ALL the gear that a Pop Warner football team would need. Oh, did I mention that the rear seat was large enough to comfortably hold 3 large football line backers.

Well, that old land yacht served the district well, and with a few more hundred miles, I was rewarded with a new high speed rocket with wheels. A brand new shiny Dodge Cornet, that did not require a booster seat or pedal extenders.

No hard feelings to the training staff, it was all taken in stride and their excellent training was much appreciated and essential to my successful career.

ACE Plate

Bob Ticer #4490

Back in the day, my road partner, Officer Jim Congrove #4776, and I were working hard to get our ACE plates. We worked in Yavapai County, and granted there were stolen vehicles up there, they were not quite as prevalent as Maricopa County and south, so we had to work pretty hard to find them. We needed to get five occupied stolens in the calendar year to receive the coveted plate, which was actually a nice Arizona copper plate with our badge number. As the year was lengthening, we were both close to getting the magic number and actively hunting the stolen cars. The competitiveness between Jim and I was growing!

One afternoon, Jim and I stopped at the State Route 69/Walmart intersection to talk with one of our squad mates who was working the road construction job when Jim had to run to use the roadside restroom (porta Jon). Why, I don't know? Either way, Flagstaff OP COMM radioed that a Yavapai County Sheriff's Deputy was out with a minor crash involving a stolen vehicle south on 89 near Kirkland. Knowing that our DPS mission was to assist other agencies and being the responsive officer that I was, I quickly grabbed the radio and said I was responding. From the porta Jon I could hear Jim yelling something at me, but I ignored him, quickly jumped in my car, and raced through Prescott down the White Spars, finally arriving with the young Deputy on the County Road, off the highway. The Deputy had the stolen vehicle suspect in his Sheriff's car and it seemed that he was unsure about investigating the crash and wasn't super interested in transporting him back to Prescott. Sensing this, I asked the Deputy if he wanted me to take the county wreck and take the suspect off his hands since he was nearing the end of his shift. The Deputy thought this was a very nice gesture and agreed to take me up on my offer.

As I turned onto State Route 89 heading north to the jail with my stolen vehicle suspect and my ACE plate goal completed, I waived at Jim as he was still southbound heading to the call. He just shook his head at me. Later that month Jim got his fifth stolen vehicle, but that is another story for sure...

Don't Become Routine

Richard Richardson #188

During 1961, three academies were scheduled, with 73 men hired out of 1,700 applicants. The classes were divided into three sessions: Class #1, Class #2, and Class #3. The first two classes would start and conclude during 1961. The third Class started Feb 1962. I was in Class #3 with 22 other cadets. graduation dinner, June 2, 1962, was at the

Holiday Restaurant-Manor on East Camelback Road, Phoenix.

Completing 16 weeks of intense training was the highlight of each of us and becoming Arizona Highway Patrolmen was special. The classroom lectures and the physical training made us better men. Each of us had special memories of those seemingly long days, listening to the various lecturers. The one thing that always comes to my mind about those days was one special thing. I still to this day think about what one lecturer said in class. Well, most said the same thing, but not as alimentally as Lt. Harley Thompson AHP #805. He stressed this point many times. What was that point? "Don't become routine!" We heard it over and over. Maybe that is why each of us knew it so well. Being routine was usually when the patrolman is at a high risk of danger. Becoming complacent can hurt you when you least expect it. Always be alert for the unexpected and you just might make it to retirement age with the department.

When I came on the AHP, only one officer had died on duty, Louis Cochran. Now look at the long list of those that paid the ultimate price.

He was very serious when he mentioned that phrase many times. The Lieutenant was a good speaker and able to hold our attention very well. His jokes were the tops of all instructors. I don't think I ever heard the same joke twice. Thanks Harley for who you were in those days, Class #3 will never forget.

The same phrase goes to every patrolman with the DPS, always remember "Don't become routine!"

They Stopped!

Roger Vanderpool #2694

My first duty station was Kayenta, the middle of the Navajo Reservation (lucky me). Officers stationed on the reservation would take their patrol vehicles to Cortez, Colorado to the Ford dealer for service. The dealer was really nice to us. We would get there when they opened and they would give us a loaner vehicle so we could go get groceries, go to a movie and get something to eat. We would return before they closed and pick up our patrol car and travel back to Kayenta. When we took our patrol vehicle for service we would wear our class C uniforms and normally took our wife along with us, since it was a big deal to go to a real town.

One morning while on our way to Cortez, with my wife, both looking forward to spending the day off the reservation, the hot tone went off, alerting us to an armed robbery that had occurred in Shiprock, New Mexico. The description of the vehicle was given and that it was last seen westbound on US 160. We were eastbound on US 160 nearing Tec Nos Pos. I knew that there wasn't anyone else 10-8 east of me. I didn't think we would see the getaway car, and then a car matching the description that had been put out passed us westbound. I told my wife that the vehicle looked like the wanted vehicle and that I needed to turn around and catch up with it and run the plate just in case. I told her it's probably not it but I need to make sure.

I caught up the vehicle and ran the plate, and the next thing I heard was the hot tone and dispatch warning me that this was the armed robbery vehicle out of Shiprock. There were four subjects in the vehicle and they were looking back to see what I was doing. I called for backup and was told that the closest units were on I-40 and in Tuba City, so I told my wife that I was going to light them up. I figured that they would do what most bad guys do and run, then we would have them heading west towards where there were some Navajo PD units enroute our way. So I hit the lights, and they STOPPED!

My wife says that as I was exiting the car with my shotgun, that I shoved her under the dash. She listened as I got the four of them out, and had them spread out on the center line. Soon after, a Graves Butane truck driver pulled up and asked me if he could help. I gave him the shotgun and told him, and the four subjects laying on the road that if any one moved to shoot the guy that isn't in uniform. The truck driver was really excited and the subjects were really scared, of the truck driver.

I got them all cuffed up and found a .38 revolver in the car. I had them sitting in the bar ditch when the PD arrived. We still made it to Cortez and enjoyed a nice lunch and movie.

Pursuit And Shooting

Bob Singer #2693

I believe it was in the summer of 1981 when I was stationed on Gray Mountain, my first duty station. I was at home in Gray Mountain when J.D. came over and said there was a pursuit coming down US89 from the north headed towards Flagstaff. J.D. (Jim) Hough, 2689, and I were classmates in the academy and had gotten assigned to Cameron together out of the academy. In October of 1980, the new ADOT yard and houses were finished in Gray Mountain where we moved. J.D. had a scanner so I went over to his house to see what was going on. What I found out later was that Officer Keith Judd from Fredonia stopped a vehicle for speed on US89A. After getting out of his patrol car and walking up to the vehicle, it took off. Keith got back in his patrol car and called in the pursuit. As he was pursing the vehicle, Flagstaff dispatch advised him that the vehicle was stolen.

At some point in the pursuit past the SR 160 turnoff to Tuba City going southbound on US 89, a passenger in the right front of the vehicle (who supposedly was an innocent hitch hiker) stuck his arm out of the car side window and fired shots at Keith's patrol car.

Back to the present time. The latest radio transmission was that they were approaching Gray Mountain where Don Voaks was going to try to shoot a shotgun slug round through the radiator of the stolen vehicle. He missed, hitting the hood instead, and the pursuit went on.

Since I was supposed to go on duty in 30 minutes, I went back home, got my uniform on and checked 10-8 and started south on US 89. Within a minute or two, I heard that the car had pulled over off of the highway and stopped. Seconds later I heard someone broadcast "998 shots fired". I don't remember the milepost but it was south of Hanks Trading Post. About a minute later, I heard someone call dispatch and say code 4 and that was all. I kept going and arrived about 10 minutes later. Our Ranger helicopter had landed just outside of the right of way fence and there were three patrol cars behind the stolen vehicle and one just to the left side of it. The three cars behind were Keith's, Don Voaks, Officer Andy Planeta from Flagstaff who had a reserve with him and Lt. Mike Osterfield's car on the left of the stolen car.

There were two bodies laying on the ground where the paramedic from the Ranger crew had checked them. It turns out that the car was incapacitated by .223 caliber rounds fired from the Ruger mini 14 the paramedic in the helicopter used, through the hood into the engine. When the cars stopped, the driver got out and started shooting at the officers behind his car and was killed by return fire.

Lt. Osterfield had just pulled up as the shooting started and fired one 00 buckshot round from his shotgun that reportedly killed the passenger who stayed in the car. After quickly looking over the situation, I told Lt. Osterfield that no one had said the suspects were dead so he called dispatch and said "we have two suspects that are 10-7".

The next day, Major Mildebrant came up from Phoenix. I got a call from my Sgt. that I was going on a special assignment. Several of us were going to walk the highway from where Keith said the passenger had shot at him on US 89 back to Cameron to search for the gun that the passenger fired out of the window. Keith said he thought he saw the passenger throw it out the window. I believe it was Jerry Deihl who was driving with the Major in the front passenger side, I was sitting on the right rear passenger side and I think Officer Mark Hall on the left rear passenger side. We walked the road for two or three miles with two of us on each side of the road in civilian clothes looking for a handgun but never found one. When we got back to Cameron, it was decided we would go off the highway and look under the bridge that crosses the Little Colorado River. We drove down a narrow dirt road that had a sharp drop off down to the river on our right side. As we got closer to the bridge, I, being on the drop off side of the car and road, noticed we were very close to the edge and told Jerry in a loud voice. Just as I did that, the right side of the vehicle dropped off of the edge and we came to a sudden stop leaning to the right. Very carefully, Jerry and Mark opened their doors on the left side of the car and slid out holding the doors down to keep the car from leaning even more over the edge. The Major slid across the front seat and I slid across the rear seat and we both got out. WHEW. That was a close one. I went up to the Chevron gas station where there was a tow truck that was on our list and he came down and pulled the car off of the edge. We never did find a handgun, no damage to the car but I think we all had to go change our shorts.

Taking Down The Hostage Takers

Ron Bruce #2048

District 3, late one evening 1986 (I think), I got a dispatch to check out at the Sanders Port of Entry for a phone call. The dispatcher said they had received a phone call from the New Mexico State Police. They had been contacted by a Continental Trailways Bus driver, in Gallup, NM. He stated that two armed men (both ex-cons it turned out) had taken all passengers and himself hostage. No stated demands had yet been made. He was allowed to get off of the bus at a truck stop in Gallup, after telling the two men that if he did not check in with his bus dispatcher, an alarm would be "sounded". State Police told him that they would be unable to gather resources quickly enough to deal with the situation and that they would notify the Arizona Department of Public Safety, since he was going to have to stop at the port of entry anyway.

I quickly gathered fellow troopers and deputies that were in the area. That included Diane Bruce, #2457, Leo Holmes, #868 and Henry Florez 3119. An Apache County Sheriff's Office sergeant and deputy were also at hand. First, I asked if anyone there had an armored vest on, or with them. No one did. I had worn out my first Second Chance vest that my mom and I had paid for in 1977. It was pretty worn out by 1984 and I had not replaced it. I thought, you've got to be kidding me!! Not one vest amongst six peace officers!

Okay, punt time. I knew the bus arrival was imminent. I asked the Agriculture Inspection Officer to loan me his hat and jacket, that so identified him. I then explained to everyone that my plan was to try and sucker folks off of the bus and direct them into the scale office, where they would then be secured on the opposite side of the port building, in the process, hopefully gaining control of the bad guys. I removed my gun belt and tucked my 4" .357 Magnum Colt Python into the rear of my uniform pants, concealed by the jacket. I had all police vehicles moved out of sight and had troopers and deputies located in various places but where they could pretty much keep an eye on what was happening and render assistance when the time came.

Sure enough, here comes the bus. It came to a stop. I approached the hinged doorway, and it was opened by the driver. I explained that I needed him to step down, so I could inspect his driving log. I escorted him into the building and he was able to tell me where the two men were sitting and that he had an additional 42 passengers. He described what they looked like and what they were wearing to the best of his memory. I did not let him go back into the bus.

Now, I went to the bus and climbed the steps into the interior. I was able to quickly identify the bad guys from the information the bus driver had provided. They were about half way back on the right side as I faced the rear. I put on my best "Welcome to Arizona, I'm the Fruit and Vegetable Inspector" face and said…paraphrased. Good evening folks, I'm Inspector Bruce and we will be conducting the standard every third bus inspection tonight. If you will gather your carry-on belongings and exit the bus, please then go through the door on the right of the building. After your items are inspected, you will be able to use a restroom and purchase food and drink items from the vending machines there. Your cooperation is appreciated. Please do this now. I stepped back down onto the asphalt and started counting heads and watching for the bad guys. Yep, it was working. At least for a short while. As I counted #30, the exit stopped. I thought, uh oh, what's going on?

I re-entered the bus. My two bad guys were perched on the edge of their seat and looking pretty agitated. There were ten black folks sitting in the back of the bus. Seriously. So I did my goofy aw come guys, let's get the show on the road so we can get you all on your way and waved my hand in encouragement. The younger of the two bad guys stood up and started towards me. I quickly stepped back to the asphalt and as he stepped down, withdrew my Colt and gave him a solid thwack on the back of his head with the barrel, which rendered him unconscious. As he fell to the ground, Diane and Henry came running towards us, to control the younger bad guy. I quickly re-entered the bus again, finding the older of the bad guys, starting to remove a Browning Hi-Power 9mm from a bag. I screamed, "Get down, I want the white guy!". All of those ten black folks did just as I had requested. I had a clean shot on Mr. Older Bad Guy and told him to drop the gun or I was going to kill him. He did just that and I escorted him from the bus, where Apache County Sheriff's Office took him into custody.

When it was all said and done I thought I was going to throw up because I was quite sure I was going to be killed.

Unbeknownst to me, District Command Staff put me in for the DPS Medal of Valor. However, an individual in the agency who did not care much for me, had the influence to quash that and the District had to settle for a Meritorious Service medal. Even still I was surprised when that was presented to me by Lt. Don Miller at a District meeting sometime after this incident. In closing, none of us did the things we did, thinking we were going to get a medal out of it. Any more than Soldiers, Sailors, Airmen or Marines do when they are in combat. Like most, when they've survived harrowing situations, I was just glad to be alive and with no new holes in my body.

Just Another Day At Work

Dick Lewis #176

We all can recall experiences and incidents we were involved in over the years. As we recall one, another comes to mind.

I was station in Globe from 1960 until 1970. We were very busy all of the time it seemed. There were only five of us to cover a large area. We were on call and were called out quite often at night during a week. We really sacked up the hours, and comp time hadn't been invented yet! Actually, we worked six days a week and did reports and vehicle maintenance on our own time.

I was a Field Training Officer and every time there was a cadet class I had a cadet for field training for a couple of weeks. Then when they graduated and if one was assigned to the Globe area, I was assigned to break him in. (To show him how it was REALLY DONE on the road.)

Well, this time Bob Martin was riding along with me and we were on the evening shift from Miami, west.

One afternoon a guy was traveling through Globe in a stolen car. He stopped in Globe and robbed, at gun point, a men's clothing store. A good description of him and the vehicle was broadcast and he was headed west. We all were looking out for him and late in the evening I jumped him coming out of the Castle Dome road, headed west. He pulled out right in front of me! Well, he ran, and the high-speed chase was on.

Faye Cooper was on radio in Carpool. She called Frank Healy who was working in Superior. Frank got set up just west of the Top of The World. As the person came into his view, Frank got in front of him. So, we had him sandwiched between us, at high speed of course.

As we were coming into Devil's Canyon going west, he started to stop. Frank was in the lead and I was behind. I popped my door and started to get out when the violator gunned it and got out around Frank. Frank gunned it and stayed with him side by side, Frank in the opposite lane. They were running side by side westbound into the canyon. As they started out of the canyon westbound the violator sideswiped Frank. Man, the sparks flew, but Frank stayed with him but had to back off and pull into Oak Flats because of oncoming traffic.

I called Frank on the radio and said, "Are you OK Frankie?" He replied back, "Yeah, go get him." I was still on the violators rear bumper as we started down the grade to the Superior Tunnel.

Jim Eaves was working west of Superior and had been listening to the chase. He came in and set up at the west end of Superior. I had cut off my top lights so the violator would slow down. He had sideswiped two other vehicles before he went through the tunnel. The violator did slow down as he went through town. Jim saw us coming and tried to get in front and turn on his lights. Well, the chase was on again!

The road west of Superior was still two lanes from Superior to Florence Junction. Here we go, top speed, all three of us. Bob Martin was running my radio. Faye Cooper (Rice) was doing a great job helping us out, letting everyone know how it was going.

We hit the divided road at the Florence Junction just boiling. Jim and I were trying to get ahead of the violator but he wouldn't let us, by switching from one lane to the other. We were still rolling towards Apache Junction at top speed. This area still was not developed and was just desert.

Patrolman Mac McCarthy was working in the Apache Junction area and started towards us. Mac said on the radio, "I'm going to shoot him." He told us on the radio how he was going to do it. "I will set up in the median at Kings Ranch Road and I will be shooting away from the eastbound road. I am going to shoot his radiator."

So, as we approached Mac, Jim and I fell back and turned off our top lights so Mac could shoot. BANG! We heard the shot and the violator gunned it. Mac jumped on the radio and said very loudly, "I missed." Faye Cooper said, "Mac missed." The race was on again!

As we rolled closer to the Junction and could see the lights, I told Jim, "Let's turn out our lights so he would slow down again and not endanger the other traffic. So, we did, and the violator slowed down.

The Pinal County deputies were waiting for us at the junction of US60 and SR88. As the violator rolled up to the junction, he turned up SR88, the road to Roosevelt, and rolled to a stop. The word came out from somewhere "He ran out of gas."

But then the foot chase began out through the desert. He was captured shortly and put in the lock up. No one was injured during this entire time.

Well, that's the story of the chase and capture. The guy was a really bad hombre, but the is another story for another time.

(Note: I didn't realize that this was such an epic event until just as I was writing it up just now. It was just another day at work for the time.)

Welcome To 1967

Doug Kluender #363

December 31, 1966: My last day of the break-in at my first duty station working with Dick Lewis in Globe AZ.

Tomorrow I will be on my own as a brand-new Highway Patrolman. That particular night we were working 2 man cars on Hwy. 70 with Lt. Phillips and Rick Ulrich in one, with Lewis and me in the other.

The bars had just closed. The first car we stopped blocked the cattle guard on the tribal road at Cutter. If Tribal members were able to get off of Hwy. 70 and on to the Tribal route here, they would be out of our jurisdiction and home free.

It was quite a traffic jam so we summoned the Tribal Police with their paddy wagon to help with all of the prisoners. The Tribal Officers were disinclined to help with loading up our prisoners so we had to "cuff 'em & stuff' 'em" in the wagon. The last 2 prisoners were trouble, a Tribal Council member & his wife.

Henry, the Councilman knew Dick Lewis and said, "no white man is going to put me in my jail without a fight". Dick made show of taking off his hat, coat, and gun belt while Henry continued to taunt him calling him "Loose". Meanwhile Rick crouched around behind Henry. Dick surprised Henry & pushed him over backwards. That took the fight out of him, so Dick & Rick were able to get him handcuffed and into the wagon.

"How Much Cyanide Gas Does It Take To...?"

Bill Hansen #2055

First, I'll start with some background. My stepdad Walt Smith (Phoenix P.D. Serial #659) transferred to the Phoenix Police Department after previously serving with the Douglas Police department in 1959. Walt's first day out of the Phoenix PD Academy was on Christmas day of 1959.

After three years on the department, Walt transferred to the Phoenix PD Detective Bureau. In the Spring of 1963, Walt's Sergeant Ed Smith (no relation) assigned him to attend an execution at the prison in Florence Arizona. As it was then, it is the norm today that executions require attendance from a cross section of society. Attendees include relatives of the victim(s), relatives of the convicted, a clergy member, a member of the media, a representative of the prosecuting agency and normally a member of the investigation team. Back in the day, the official invitation for an execution was send out in a manner that was similar to a printed wedding invitation.

I remember Walt telling me that the execution was performed shortly after midnight on March 14,

1963 with no fanfare. He also recalled that the condemned inmates last meal consisted of several fried chickens and ice cream for dessert.

As it turned out, this execution was the last execution in Arizona until 1992.

Fast forward to the Spring of 1992, I was a member of the DPS Bomb Squad and the DPS Hazardous Materials Team. I was attending a meeting at the Arizona Department of Environmental Quality (ADEQ), going over a case that we had worked after a train derailment had released hazardous chemicals into the environment. While in the meeting, I was seated at the desk of ADEQ First Responder Mike Malone (retired USAF Bomb Tech) and the phone rang. Mike answered the phone and after a few moments he replied, "Who is this….?" Mike stated "Hold on, I'll put you on speaker." After placing the phone on speaker, he introduced me and said go ahead with your question. The caller said, this is Captain (I don't recall his name) at the prison in Florence. The Captain said, "we have an execution coming up in less than a month and we don't have anyone employed here that has ever executed anyone!" His question was, "How Much Cyanide Gas Does It Take To Kill Someone?" Mike and I looked at each other bewildered to say the least! The Captain then stated, "while attempting a dry run, there had been a bit of an incident." When we inquired what the incident involved he said, "they

used cyanide powder under the execution chair to test the remote actuator."
The actuator would drop the cyanide tablet into a vat of acid during the actual execution. He said, "the incident occurred when the fan located under the seat of the chair flung powder all over and into the execution chamber. At this time, we asked what type of cyanide had been used in the test. The captain replied, "that they had purchased 25 pounds of Potassium Cyanide powder." The Captain included, that during the process of purchasing cyanide, the ADOC purchaser had ordered on low-bid powdered potassium cyanide. At this point we realized the Arizona Department of Corrections was going to need some assistance. First, we informed the captain that they had acquired the incorrect type of Cyanide. We explained to him that the correct cyanide required for the execution would be sodium cyanide and it needed to be in tablet form.

We were asked by the Captain what should be done with the 25 pounds of the potassium cyanide? We had contacts with the copper mining industry in Arizona and we were able to give the Potassium Cyanide to the mines in the area, as they use it in large quantities. We then directed our attention with the purchasing department with the prison and we were able to locate and order by special delivery, sodium cyanide tablets and Hydrochloric acid. (HCL)

In 1963 the U.S. Environmental Protection Agency had not been created. When the preparations were being completed for this execution, Mike Malone told me that we had another obstacle to overcome. The process of neutralizing of the hydrogen cyanide gas in the chamber prior to entry would be necessary. To neutralize the HCL gas, ammonia gas will be piped into the chamber. Mike then advised, the residual gas would be removed from the chamber by flowing fresh air into the chamber and venting the exhaust gas out through the roof of the death house into the atmosphere. Mike was able to obtain an environmental hazardous waste permit to allow the staff to vent the chamber.

To prepare the ADOC entry team personnel for entry into the chamber after the execution, we conducted training with the selection and proper donning and doffing of Personal Protective Equipment (PPE) and the use of Air Purifying Respirators (APR's).

We found old documentation that up to the last execution in 1963, the Prison entry team would wear WWII gas masks as the only PPE worn and they had no remote monitoring equipment to determine the levels of Hydrogen Cyanide gas in the chamber. In those days, they only had a stethoscope to determine if the inmate was deceased unlike today, where they are able to monitor the condemned remotely and know when he, or she has died from the execution.

Unknown to Mike and myself, the ADOC Director Sam Lewis, had been monitoring the entire process of the execution and had become very involved in the process. When he caught word of the hiccups that were occurring in the process understandably, he had become very concerned. The Captain had communicated through his chain of command how he had received assistance in this assignment from representatives from the Arizona Department of Environmental Quality and the Arizona Department of Public Safety. The word came down shortly afterward from DPS Director Ayars that in addition to the DPS D-6 personnel that had been scheduled to perform duties for this event, Director Lewis requested Bomb Squad, Haz Mat and AZ DEQ folks to be on site as a precaution.

Incidentally, our attendance continued for several years and while involved in another execution, I ran into DPS Lt Bill Breen. Early in his career as a Cochise County Sheriff's Sergeant, Bill had investigated a murder and had followed the case through all of the court proceeding, appeals and finally after 15 years, or so attended the execution of his arrestee. Bill will be writing an article in this issue describing his investigation and all of the proceedings following the case through appeals.

Since this was the first execution in almost 30 years, it was interesting to see the different types of protesters present. In the five or six executions that I attended, it became common to see outside of the prison at the designated public demonstration area Pro-Execution, Anti-Execution protesters along with the venders selling "Hang em High" type t-shirts, hats and coffee cups. There were also those selling bibles and praying that the execution be halted.

The executions were completed without incident.....Interesting times....indeed!

From The Beginning To The End

Bill Breen #3407

This multiple murder case was investigated by a number of investigators, including DPS Agent Herman Flores #228, Cochise County Corporal Bill Cloud (later to become DPS Detective #3408) and Cochise County Sheriff's Sgt. Bill Breen (later to become DPS Lt. #3407). Retired DPS Major Ron Mayes #225 arranged for Lt. Breen to be a witness to the execution.

It was on the night of December 4, 1977 that four people were murdered in their beds at the Cochise Guest Ranch & Lodge, located in Elfrida, Arizona. The owners, Charles Thumm and Mildred Thumm were each shot in the head multiple times in their modest ranch house. Two ranch hands, fifty-one-year-old George Martin and young seventeen-year-old Gerry McFerron, were killed as they slept in their beds in the bunkhouse. Martin was stabbed seven times in the chest and young Gerry McFerron was shot multiple times in the head.

The ranch was a gruesome scene of dead bodies and blood.

One other ranch employee, twenty year old James Dean Clark of Jackson, Michigan, was missing. Also missing were a saddle, jewelry, credit cards, guns, cash and the Thumm's station wagon.

Sheriff Jim Judd, Chief Deputy Doug Knipp, myself and sheriff's detectives responded to the scene. The Sheriff contacted the Arizona Department of Public Safety and requested the assistance of DPS Agent Herman Flores. The Cochise County officers considered Herman Flores one of the most thorough investigators in the entire state of Arizona. His ability to carefully process difficult and intricate crime scenes made him a highly respected detective.

As the officers all worked under Agent Flores' direction and supervision to process the scene, remove the bodies, dust for fingerprints and photograph everything, a search began for James Dean Clark. After the scene was secured and processed, the Sheriff told me and Corporal Bill Cloud to "Find James Dean Clark!" Thus began an extended, round-the-clock search for twenty year old Clark, now a prime suspect in four brutal, bloody murders.

Cloud and I began our search by putting out an "Attempt to locate" bulletin to law enforcement agencies nationwide for Clark and the Thumm's station wagon. We also worked closely with the security offices of Visa and MasterCard, to trace any use of the Thumm's credit cards.

A break came when I received a call from the Visa credit card security folks. They advised a young man was in a jewelry store in the Bassett Shopping Center in El Paso, Texas. He was purchasing a diamond ring with the Thumm's Visa credit card. The security folks said the suspect was standing in front of the store clerk at that very moment.

When the security people gave me that information, I told them to tell the clerk to try to stall the man until El Paso Police could get there. The clerk relayed through the Visa people that the suspect had left the store and agreed to come back to the store at 4:30 P.M. to pick up the ring. I then called the jewelry store clerk and got a physical description of the suspect. Her description of the suspect matched that of Clark. El Paso Police Department's Homicide Division was called and I briefed an El Paso detective on the case and that the suspect was going to return to the jewelry store in just two hours.

The detective assured me he would take care of it and would call back when the suspect was in custody. Three hours later, I still had not heard from El Paso, so I called the Homicide Division again and asked for the detective. I was informed that the detective had gone off duty at 4 P.M. and was now at home! The officers in Homicide had no knowledge of the homicide or that the suspect was in their city! The detective never gave the information to anyone and no one had gone to the jewelry store! I found out later the suspect had returned to the store, picked up the ring and left! El Paso Police command staff and an Assistant Chief got an ear-full from me and I was assured they would find Clark and would keep the Cochise County Sheriff's office informed. Eventually, they found the Thumm's station wagon parked next to the border crossing with Juarez, Chihuahua, Mexico.

The El Paso officers remained on surveillance throughout the night watching the station wagon. Then they saw him: a man matching the description of Clark walking back into the U.S. They watched as the man approached the station wagon, unlocked the door and got in. The officers surrounded the vehicle and removed the suspect at gunpoint. The man was James Dean Clark. The car was full of Thumm's belongings, including the saddle and the murder weapons. Clark had the stolen credit cards on him.

After Clark was placed in a jail cell, it was learned he had unsuccessfully tried to sell the stolen saddle at the El Paso County Sheriff's Office! He also came into contact with a heroin addict who had been working as an informant for the DEA. According to the informant, Clark had bragged that he had killed four people in Arizona. The informant told officers that Clark told him, "You should have seen Charlie (Charles Thumm) when I hit him with those wadcutters!"

Clark waived extradition and was flown back to Arizona to stand trial for four counts of first degree murder and robbery.

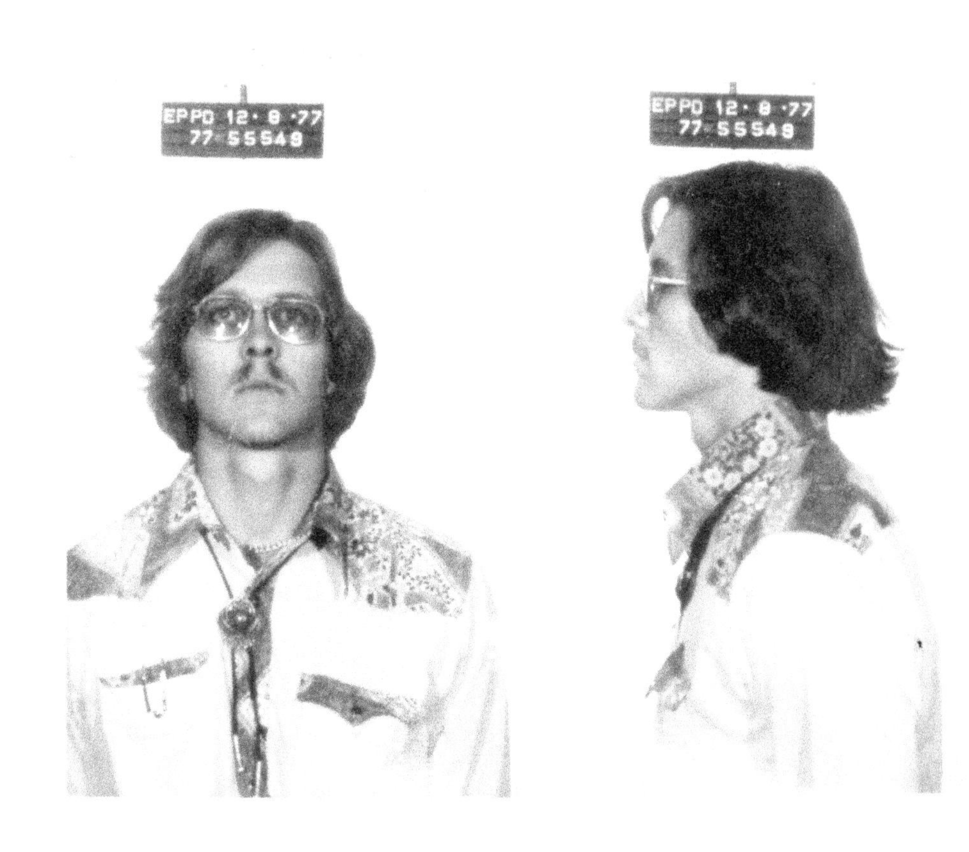

Murderer: James Dean Clark

The trial was presided over by Cochise County Superior Judge Anthony T. Deddens. After a short deliberation by the jury, Clark was found guilty of all charges.

At the sentencing, Deddens sentenced Clark to die for his crimes. As the judge passed sentence, Clark stood and smirked. He never showed any remorse for his crimes and didn't seem to care that he was sentenced to die.

Clark was transferred to the Arizona State Prison, where he remained throughout his many court appeals over the years. Each time an appeal was raised, the Supreme Court would eventually deny each appeal. During the course of these appeals, Judge Deddens retired from the bench and later died. James Dean Clark remained very much alive, sitting on "Death Row" at the State Prison in Florence, Arizona.

After many years of appeals, the Supreme Court of the United States finally denied Clark's last appeal in 1993. Alan Polley, the Cochise County Attorney in 1993, contacted me (I was a DPS detective lieutenant, by then) asking me to assist the County Attorney and the Arizona Attorney General's Office in the Clemency Hearing to be conducted the day of Clark's scheduled execution.

I had been involved in the case throughout the years, and was going to be a witness at the clemency hearing at the State Prison on the day of the scheduled execution. I then reached out to retired DPS Major Ron Mayes, who was then working for Dept. of Corrections Director Sam Lewis. As a result, four days before Clark's scheduled execution, I received a letter from Director Sam Lewis, informing me that I had been selected as one of the witnesses to the execution of James Dean Clark.

The Governor's Office issued a Death Warrant for James Dean Clark, ordering the Warden of the Arizona State Prison to carry out the death sentence on April 13, 1993. On that date, I testified before the Arizona Board Of Pardons And Paroles as to the facts surrounding the four murders. After hearing testimony from me and others, it was going to be up to the seven members of this Board to decide whether to give clemency to James D. Clark, and give him life without parole or allow the death sentence to be carried out.

Remembering the bloody crime scene from sixteen years ago, I testified to the facts of the case. One of Mr. Clark's attorney's, Robert Hooker, tried very hard to convey to the Board that Clark was a changed man and that the investigation of the homicides had been bungled, resulting in an innocent man (Mr. Clark) being wrongly placed on "Death Row."

A short time later, the Board of Pardons and Paroles re-convened. They unanimously voted against Clark's bid for clemency. The Governor was notified of the Board's decision and the Governor concurred that the death sentence would be carried out. I attended the execution, which was carried out a few hours later, just before midnight.

It had been fifteen years and four months from the crime to the final punishment.

A Patrol Car With A Speed Limiter?????

Bob Singer #2693

It was sometime in the summer of 1990 when I was stationed in Springerville. We were living in a cute log cabin in Eagar near the rodeo grounds where US 666 (now US 191) comes from the south from Alpine, goes into Springerville and connects with US 60 that goes to ShowLow. It was just before 8am, my 10-8 time. When I got into my patrol car and checked 10-8 with Flagstaff radio, the dispatcher greeted me and said there was a white Geo Prizm that had just skipped paying for gas at the only gas station in Alpine and was headed north on US 666. From my driveway next to the road, I could see triple 6 as it went south and up the side of the mountain for several miles. I figured that would be the best place to wait for the car. After about 15 minutes, I saw a small white car coming down the hill northbound toward me so I notified radio that I believed I had the car in sight. As the white Geo Prizm passed me, I put my new patrol car, a 1989 Ford Crown Victoria, into drive and pulled out behind the Prizm.

I noticed that there was an early 20's white male driver and an early 20's white female passenger in the front. Getting close enough to see the license plate, I called dispatch and had her run the plate. Within several seconds, dispatch called me back, "2693, 10-40" (A stolen vehicle). I replied "10-4" and turned on my lights and siren. The Prizm had been going the speed limit but when I turned on my lights and siren, it took off. I called dispatch and told them I was now in pursuit, and would she call the Apache County Sheriff's Office dispatcher to let them know because they also dispatched the Springerville and Eager PD. When we got to the "T" intersection of triple 6 and US 60 on the east side of Springerville, the Prizm turned left onto US 60 but spun out and came to a stop. I put my car in park and started to get out drawing my pistol but the car turned around and accelerated west through town. Getting back into my patrol car, I followed, lights and siren blaring through town and west on US 60.

It was easy for my trusty patrol car to keep up with the little four cylinder Geo Prizm going up and down the small hills west of Springerville but unknown to me, a surprise was in store for me. While this was going on, Flagstaff dispatch had called the ShowLow office and gotten a hold of Lt. DeBoer, our District Commander, to let him know what was happening. He and a couple of the officers from that area went east to set up a roadblock just west of the ShowLow, Springerville and St. Johns SR 61 junction.

Now back to me. As we went up the dormant volcano summit just east of Vernon, I was very close to the Prizm with the power of my Ford and the lack of power of the little Prizm. When we reached the top of the summit and started down the west side, the Prizm's speed quickly picked up and we soon reached 105 mph. Suddenly, the engine of my trusty Ford quit. I looked at the gages and everything seemed ok but putting my foot all the way down to the floor on the gas pedal didn't do anything. When the car's speed dropped down to 95, it suddenly accelerated again but when it got to 105, it quit again. The little Prizm was quickly pulling away from me. I called dispatch and told her what was happening. When I reached the bottom of the summit and got to Vernon, the Prizm was out of sight. From that point on, I kept the Ford at 100 mph so it wouldn't stop again. At a point about 2 miles from the ShowLow, Springerville, St. Johns junction I could see the roadblock but still couldn't see the Prizm. It was at that time that Lt. DeBoer called me on the radio and asked me where the Prizm was. I told him that if he couldn't see it, it had probably turned east onto SR61 towards St. Johns. Fortunately, Ron Lewis was waiting at the roadblock in his fast little Ford Mustang so he took off to find the Prizm on SR61. I also took the SR61 turnoff to try to catch up.

Ron had caught up to the Prism before they reached Concho and was giving updates on milepost locations. After going through Concho, the Prizm took a dirt road that went off of the left side of SR 61. Ron called and said the Prizm had taken that road. The next thing I heard from Ron was that the Prizm had crashed into a berm at a "T" intersection and he was going to be in foot pursuit. I got there within about 30 seconds and saw that Ron had a female in handcuffs. He pointed to my left and ahead to indicate where the male had run. I drove past the high berm of the road and saw the male suspect had jumped a barbed wire fence and was running across a field about 25 yards in front of me. Not knowing if he had a gun, I drew my shotgun out of my scabbard and yelled for him to stop and put his hands up. He did as I instructed. I had him walk back to me while I covered him with my shotgun, climb over the fence and I took him into custody. I then transported both of them to the Apache County jail where they were booked on several charges. Ron stayed for the tow truck and did the accident report if I remember correctly.

The next day, I stopped by the little Ford dealership in Springerville and told them what had happened with the car's engine quitting at 105 mph. The head mechanic told me that they all have speed governors built into the engine control management (ECM) computer to limit the cars speed. REALLY, on a Police car? I then told Chris Ryder, my Sergeant in Springer and Lt. DeBoer about the problem with the ECM. I don't believe anything was ever done about it. Within a couple of months, Larry Parks on my squad got promoted to Sergeant and went to Yuma so I got his Mustang. It DID NOT have a speed limiter.

Every Dog Has His Day

Bill Rogers #3578

A gas station convenience store on US60 in Miami catered to the long-haul truckers. The problem was, it didn't offer convenient parking for the semi-tractor trailers that drove into it. There were marked parking spaces for cars parallel to the highway that the truckers could use several of, which they often did. Under the federal law for commercial vehicles, which I was schooled by DPS in, I could stop and inspect truck tractors. I would often see minor traffic violations when these trucks parked there, which invited me to contact the drivers and introduce myself.

On one occasion I saw a truck driver pull over and park near the gas station. He exited his truck and was gone over ten minutes away from his vehicle in the store area. Federal law requires the placement of road reflectors if parked on the roadside over ten minutes. The reflectors were missing, so I had an invitation. I grabbed my clipboard that retained my copy of the Driver

Vehicle Examination Report and walked up to the driver's door of the big rig. I was copying down the DOT number and other information off the truck's door when the driver reappeared from the store area.

Now truck drivers are notorious for their poor health and being overweight. I mean no disrespect since my father was a truck driver. I know all too well the horrors of the job. But this man was the roundest driver I had ever seen. He was about six feet tall and about six feet in diameter. I honestly wondered how the guy even fit in the cab, visualizing that from door to doghouse it must have been filled to overflowing.

I asked for the usual paperwork and allowed the driver to climb into the cab of the truck. He put the bags of food from the gas station into the sleeper. I acquired the logbook, registrations, license and related paperwork before conducting the commercial vehicle inspection. Once this was done, I ordered the driver to the rear of his truck where I could complete all the mounds of paperwork he had created for me.

It was then that I noticed that a City of Miami police officer had arrived on the scene. Now, Miami was a very small city, and having more than two officers on duty at once was unusual. They also usually employed very young, inexperienced officers and this was no exception. He was skinny and had that rookie look of still being excited about being a cop. I figured that the truck driver could eat this officer's weight in one sitting. We conversed for a moment as he was curious about my stop and wanted to check on my safety. I appreciated his offer.

I had the driver stand facing me at the rear of his truck, off the roadway, away from traffic. His logbook was extremely behind and I placed him out of service for eight hours. I explained to him where to park his truck after I completed my business with him. I cited him for several other commercial violations. It was going to be a very costly experience for him.

I remember the next few moments as they are fearfully etched in my memory bank. I was feeling cocky, kinda showing off in a non-expressive way to the young city officer. He stood to my right, watching my every move. I had my clipboard in my hand holding the pound of paperwork I had just completed. The driver had never been threatening, but more of less resigned to his fate. I had my head down just starting to look up when the driver spoke.

"Are we done? Thanks." That's all I heard. Then I saw his huge right hand extended to shake hands. I took my pen from my right hand to my left shirt pocket and gripped his hand. Then I wish I never had.

The giant was strong and had a vise grip I had never felt before, nor to this day. All the work on the truck had made him genuinely strong beyond belief. I had been standing an arm's length away when he pulled my noodle arm. He lifted me off of my feet in one jerk as he brought his hand to his heart. He retained a death grip on my hand and I followed that direction. I stood on tiptoes as we were now face to face. I smelled his rancid breath.

The driver twisted his lips into action and told me, "Just remember, every dog has his day." And then, just as quick he released me, turned, and was climbing into his truck. I watched the truck pull away from the curb before I could even take a breath. I tried to regain composure, as I still had the rookie watching me.

The rookie spoke first, "Damn, I thought I was going to have to shoot him," I kinda nodded, making my way quickly to my patrol car. I turned the air conditioner on full blast. I finally started breathing regularly and felt my heart start beating again.

I was just as scared at that moment by the trucker's actions as I have ever been. I was completely out of defensive or offensive position, completely at his mercy, unable to save myself. I swore to never be that cocky again. It was a lifelong lesson I will never forget.

Felony Code 34

Colin Peabody #481

I graduated from the AHP Academy on April 26, 1968, after 16 weeks of training that included having Courteous Vigilance drilled into us recruits, along with our duty to tend to disabled motorists (Code 34s), some drug and drug addict identification films mixed in with traffic codes and accident investigation.

My very first shift by myself started at 3 PM on a Sunday afternoon, working US66 west of Winslow. I made my way west of town and about 10 miles out, I see a 62 Chevy II parked off the highway on the south shoulder in a wide pullout. Being a new and very conscientious Highway Patrolman, eager to perform my sworn duty to assist a motorist, I pulled in parallel to the driver's side of the Chevy and looked over to see an elderly gray haired man sitting in the right front passenger seat, leaning forward towards the dashboard. As I looked closer, I see he has a functioning lighter on the open glove box door, he is holding a spoon with a bent handle over the flame of the lighter. I knew from my recent training that he was cooking an illegal substance in that spoon.

I yelled at him to stop as I bailed out of my car, he yelled back "Remember your Madre!" I yelled back "My mother doesn't do drugs!". By then I have his door open and I am pulling him out of the car and quickly patting him down , then cuffing him. I had him sitting on the ground when I noticed two things, the spoon had a white substance in the bowl of the spoon, a syringe and there was a female either sleeping or passed out in the back street. I even remembered to read him his Miranda rights. I secured him in the front seat of

my car and called Holbrook for assistance and to have Sgt. Bob Harvey notified.
A few minutes later, I had the female out of the car and sitting on the ground when Sgt. Harvey and my academy mate Ron DeLong showed up. I told the Sgt. I wasn't sure what I had but suspected the old guy was cooking heroin, and DeLong agreed, having seen the same films I had seen, showing an addict cooking heroin in a spoon, over a lighter and using a cotton ball as a filter. Just what we had on the glovebox door.
Sgt Harvey admitted he had never experienced anything like that before in his 15 years with the Patrol, but we had him take photos that didn't turn out well.
We charged the old man, 63-year-old Anastasio Saavedra, with Possession of Dangerous Drugs and transported him to the Winslow Jail, and then to Flagstaff the next morning. We turned the female, the old man's daughter, loose. We had no way to accurately test the substance until we were able to send it to the Arizona Dept. of Law's Narcotics unit, where Cliff Vanderark tested it and determined it was heroin. Cliff and I had remembered that case together over the course of our careers after Cliff was transitioned into DPS on July 1, 1969.

The old man was a two time loser in California and once they were notified, they wanted him back for a parole violation, so we turned him over to

California. I can't verify it, but that arrest may have been one of the first heroin arrests made by an Arizona Highway Patrolman, whose primary duties were traffic enforcement.
Poor Sergeant Harvey now had his hands full with two rookies who tested his patience and knowledge with the various activities we managed to encounter while on routine patrol on Route 66. He never would have figured a Code 34 would become a felony and neither did I!

The Check Is In The Mail

Ron Cox #1101

To the best of my memory, this story began on 4/26/73. I came on duty at 0600 to relieve Jerry Boren, #524, from Safford, who had worked the graveyard shift and had the only radar unit between the Willcox area and Safford. We were parked on the E/bound side of I-10 about a half mile west of Exit 355. Exits 352 and 355 were N/bound exits for hwy 666, now 191, going to Safford. As we were standing beside the cars, a fairly slow mover came by E/bound with an expired California tag. I jumped in my car to start my day off with him as my first contact. He immediately signaled to take exit 355 when I fell in behind him. I thought this as being odd since he'd already passed exit 352. Jerry fell in behind me since we were now headed towards Safford. He told me over car to car that he'd stop too. I turned on the top mounts and the driver pulled over. Jerry pulled around in front of him. As I approached the driver's door, I could see that the guy had about everything he owned in the car, including a bulky tv set in the back seat. He asked me why I was harassing him, and I noticed a small cassette recorder in his hands. I asked him to please hand me his driver's license, which he did. I then asked him to step back to the rear of his car with me. He asked if he could bring his tape recorder with him? I told him that he could bring his tv with him if he wanted, but please come to the rear with me. By now, Jerry is out of his vehicle sort of wandering around peering into the guys windows.

The man seemed very nervous. He was trying to speak with me, but at the same time turning around watching Jerry. His name was George Sylvester Duckworth. He started in with why, was I harassing him again. "I've been harassed and stopped by you people over 200 times and I've never even been given a ticket! I'm sick and tired of this harassment!" And the recorder was running the whole time. And he's still nervous because of Jerry wandering around looking. I told him that I'd stopped him because he had an expired tag on his license plate, and that I didn't feel like that was harassment, and that I was going to give him a ticket. I gave him the citation, he got in his car, and headed towards Safford. I ran checks on him and there were no warrants, nothing. Jerry and I discussed what a strange individual he was for a few minutes, then we went our separate ways.

Fast forward to 4/29 or 4/30/73. As I recall, I was home when I received a phone call from a Texas Ranger named Grady. He'd gotten my number from DPS headquarters. He asked if I recalled stopping a man named George Duckworth. I told him yes, I clearly remembered Mr. Duckworth.

The following is what Ranger Grady told me: The morning after I made contact with Duckworth, he shot and killed a Sheriff in Marfa, Texas, and wounded a deputy. He was taken into custody by a Border Patrol agent and was in jail. Grady advised that they also had the cassette tape from my contact with Duckworth. Duckworth had pulled off the highway to sleep the night of the 26th. When he was waking up, a cowboy turned onto the road where he was parked. He stopped and asked him what he was doing there. Duckworth told him he just spent the night there in his car, and that he had the owner's permission. The cowboy knew better, because he was the ranch foreman. He drove to the ranch and called the Sheriff. The Sheriff showed up, along with a new, young deputy he was breaking in. Duckworth was sitting on the passenger side with the door open, and his feet on the ground. When the two lawmen approached him, Duckworth produced a .22 semi auto pistol from his waistband and shot the Sheriff several times. The deputy took off running, and Duckworth shot him in the shoulder at least once.

It was a short distance to the highway, and the deputy got a ride from a passerby to a BP checkpoint a few miles down the road. Border Patrol showed up, arrested Duckworth without incident, and turned him over to local authorities. During the interview with Duckworth, he admitted to the shooting and again complained about being harassed by law enforcement. Grady found the citation I'd written, and listened to the conversation on the cassette. He asked Duckworth why he didn't shoot Jerry and myself? He said that if he could have gotten the two of us together, he was planning to try to get us both. He had the pistol in his waistband covered by his shirt. It seems that George Sylvester Duckworth was a retired Air Force Major that hated authority. Those were his words to Ranger Grady.

A few months later, I received a subpoena from the State of Texas for the murder trial of George Duckworth. I was given 2 options: I could go on DPS time in a state car and turn over any expense monies from Texas to the State of Arizona, or I could take vacation time, take my wife with me, and keep expense reimbursement monies from Texas. I opted for plan #2.

To shorten things up a bit, we went to Texas, I wasn't called to testify, but my wife sat in on the trial. Needless to say, Duckworth was convicted, and died in prison about 10 years later. The BP agent that arrested Duckworth was called to the stand. (This according to my wife). The defense attorney asked him " When you arrived at the scene, did you point your weapon at Mr. Duckworth and tell him Run you son of a b_ _ _ _ , run." BP agent said "no sir." Attorney asked did anyone tell Mr. Duckworth to "run you son of a b_ _ _ _ run? BP Agent said, "why no sir, that's against our policy."

I submitted my expenses for a total of $105 to the great State of Texas, and was told that the check would be in the mail. That should have been a clue. Several weeks later I got a letter from the State of Texas. It said, as close as I can remember," a subpoena issued outside the State of Texas has no scope or authority. Therefore, you were not required to come, and we are not required to pay you anything". The letter went all the way to Major Mildebrant. He informed me that he was not happy and would do his best to get my check for me. After several more weeks, the Major called me. He'd tried anyone and everyone he knew, but Texas held their stand that they weren't paying me a dime. But the Major told me this: I can guarantee you that because of this, any subpoenas that are sent to DPS officers from out of state, if there's not a check in the envelope with it, throw it in the trash!!!

I thank Jerry Boren, may he Rest In Peace, for hanging around a few extra minutes when he didn't have to. And I thank Major Mildebrant for putting the effort into trying to help me out. May he Rest In Peace as well. I attended Jerry's funeral service and afterwards related this story to Bill Mulleneaux and his son.

The Mexico Connection

Charlie Ruiz #1267

On November 7, 1983, the Air Interdiction Squad received an alert from US Custom's Air support that they were following a target that crossed over the US/ Mexico Border east of Arizona heading north by northwest.

The squad was assigned designated clandestine airstrips to cover in case the target plane headed towards one of the strips. The target plane bypassed Phoenix still heading northwest in the direction of Parker or Kingman Arizona.

Highway Patrol units were notified to be on the lookout for suspicious vehicles exiting the desert. Soon thereafter Sergeant Tom Gosh reported that two trucks came out of the desert south of Bouse. He made the attempt to stop both vehicles by placing his vehicle between both trucks. He got the vehicles stopped and when he exited his patrol car and started to walk up to the truck, the driver gunned the car and drove back into the desert in a dry wash with lights out. The truck behind him made a quick u turn heading south. This vehicle was eventually pulled over and the driver was arrested and held at the Salome Sheriff's substation.

Upon our arrival Agent Mike Stevens and I located the area where the first truck fled into the desert. We followed the tracks in the dry wash for several miles eventually locating approximately 1400 pounds of marijuana. The driver and truck continued into the desert with lights out. The truck was found the following morning by Agent Ron Cox stuck in a ravine a few miles away. Footprints were followed to Bouse approximately 10 miles away.

The driver that was stopped by the highway patrolman was booked into the sheriff's jail in Salome, Arizona. I interviewed the driver and after a joint agreement between DPS supervisors, the US Attorney and the squad members, it was agreed to use the suspect driver as a confidential source. In true form the confidential source kept in touch with me agreeing to provide information for an arrest of equal size in the near future. On the last day of January 1984 I received a call from the CI who advised of a warehouse just south of Sell's Arizona in Mexico that was storing approximately 10 tons of marijuana. I contacted a friend from California DEA and we made arrangements for them to pick up the confidential source and fly to Arizona pick me up. We would try and locate the warehouse in Mexico. As it turned out the confidential source did not show up at the given location so the trip was canceled.

A few days later I received a call from the confidential source who advised that while he was waiting to be picked up, friends showed up at the airport. They were known Colombian drug smugglers and they asked him if he would drive a vehicle from Mexico into Brownsville Texas with the load to which he agreed. He stated that he figured I would rather make an arrest in Arizona than in Mexico.

Plans were made for the confidential source to gather intelligence on residence locations, names of people involved, locations where they were picking up the load and from where they were driving. He provided all this within a couple of weeks. I contacted my counterpart in Texas DPS, Special Agent George Olivos and provided the address of a residence in Brownsville Texas. Agent Olivo's followed through and set up surveillance units utilizing US Customs, Texas DPS and local agencies. At this time the Drug Enforcement Administration did not want to participate thinking it would never happen.

The next call I received was on February 2nd 1984 from the confidential source in the middle of the night telling me that he was in Tampico Mexico. I specifically gave him orders not to go into the Republic of Mexico because I could not give him permission. He stated that when somebody is holding a gun, you have to do what they tell you. He said he would call me at a later date with travel orders. Additional information that the confidential source provided was that that they had the load but because of bad weather and muddy roads they were unable to leave and that he would call me when he arrived in Matamoros Mexico. (Matamoros is across the river from Brownsville Texas)

The next call I received from the confidential source was on February 10th, stating that he was in Brownsville and the load was across the border in Mexico in Matamoros. The confidential source further stated that they would be crossing with the load sometime that night but didn't know exactly when or where they would be crossing. They would be using a rubber raft or a little boat and take it to the house in Brownsville where they would prepare it.

I contacted my sergeant, Colin Peabody who made arrangements with the brass to provide an airplane so that we could fly to Brownsville. We were provided the King Air with Jim Heflin as our pilot and we arrived in Brownsville Texas around 9:30 PM that day. I met up with Texas DPS sergeant Ray Coffmen and Agent George Olivos and we were taken to a motel where we would be staying. We had a brief meeting there with the agents who would be assisting. After the briefing we all headed out to our designated areas. It was getting late when sergeant Peabody and I got in the car with sergeant Coffman. At approximately 10 PM with no activity, getting nervous I ask Sgt Coffman to check and see if there was any movement. We were advised that around 8 PM a truck was loaded up with a couple of small boats and they pulled out and drove to an area by the Rio Grande and drove on a dirt road on the US side. The vehicles were in the area for approximately 30 minutes then came out and drove to suspect residence. They went into the garage and closed the door. They were still inside of the house.

At approximately 5 AM on the morning of February 11th we were notified by the surveillance units which were right across the street from the suspect residents that there was movement inside the house. The garage door opened up a vehicle which looked like a Crown Victoria pulled out and baggage was placed into the vehicle. They drove off with surveillance units following. We were waiting at an intersection outside of town when we were notified that surveillance lost the vehicles. Ironically the suspect vehicle passed right in front of us. We were the only vehicle in view of the suspects so sergeant Coffman decided to stop the vehicle before we lost it again. A traffic stop was made all subjects in the vehicle were taken into custody. We waited till the other unit arrived to assist in transporting the vehicle and subjects to the law enforcement office in Brownsville. Shortly thereafter the search warrant was executed on the residence and Brownsville vehicles and one aircraft that was parked at the Harlingen, Texas airport. Seized were the following items:

335 pounds of high-quality cocaine stored in 8 duffel bags, one twin aircraft, 3 1/2 ton pickups, two 12' boats with motors, miscellaneous items including swimsuits, and several walkie talkie radios plus $10,000 cash.

After an exhausting 2 days we managed to get back to the motel room for some well needed rest, When we arrived at 9:30 the previous day the pilot Jim Haflin asked us to wake him up when the deal was going down cause he wanted to be there. Needless to say we were unable to and to this day I think he is still mad at us for not waking him up.

In conclusion 7 Colombians were arrested, 5 males and 2 females. One of Columbians placed a contract on me and some of the other agents. It was later rescinded when the same Columbian became a confidential source for the Federal Drug Enforcement Administration.

When it was all over, Lt Reutter called us in and gave us all an attaboy. Then he turned to me and said, “Great job. Now what are you going to do tomorrow?” You gotta love Bill Reutter.

Sometimes Things Do Work Out

Colin Peabody #481

In early 1983, I was assigned to the DPS Air Interdiction Squad, assigned to work with U.S. Customs
Air Support out to Sky Harbor Airport in Phoenix. As such, our entire squad consisting of Mike Stevens #585(RIP), Bill Daily #573(RIP), Jim Paden #617(RIP), Ron Cox #1101, Charlie Ruiz #1267 and Mike " MadDog" Taylor #1271 and myself, were deputized as Deputy United States Marshals, having federal peace officer authority and jurisdiction, and able to make federal arrests in Arizona or wherever we happened to be working. It wasn't unusual to find ourselves in New Mexico, southern Utah, southern California, Nevada or even in southern Texas.

As the result of a major air smuggling case that we conducted with U.S. Customs in November 1983 in western Arizona near the Colorado River, about 1400 lbs. of marijuana, two pickup trucks and several arrests were made. One of those arrested was subsequently allowed to work as a confidential informant and he agreed to maintain contact with Charlie Ruiz #1267, with the agreement, any case he worked had to result in a major seizure. About a month went by and Charlie had contact with the informant and into January the informant was approached by a group of

Columbians to work with them on getting a load of cocaine into the US. Over the next couple of weeks, Charlie learned more about the operation and he made contact with Texas DPS Sergeant George Olivo and his supervisor, Lt. Ray Coffman. Information went back and forth between Charlie, and the Texas DPS officers as well as the informant.

The basic plan involved cocaine being brought across Mexico then to the Rio Grande in small boats, taken to a stash house in Brownsville, then taken to the airport at Harlingen, Texas, loaded onto a Beechcraft Queen Air twin aircraft and flown to Arizona for refueling, then on to the Los Angeles area. Once the informant gave specific information as to when this was going to occur, Texas DPS and the local U.S. Customs officers moved into place and kept surveillance on the suspects and their activities.

Charlie got a call early on the morning of Feb. 10, 1984, that the group was going to be moving the load that evening. He let Texas DPS know the plans and since Charlie knew the informant on sight, we were asked to fly down and assist as Texas DPS felt it necessary to us to be there and would bolster the case.

I made arrangements through our Lieutenant, Bill Reutter #621 to secure a DPS aircraft to fly to Brownsville as soon as possible. Since time was of the essence, our fastest aircraft was a Beech King Air, (N911AZ), and we requested that plane rather than the smaller, slower Beechcraft Baron. While the wheels can turn very slowly most of the time, this time, our travel plans were expedited quickly with travel orders and the use of the King Air. Charlie and I went to Sky Harbor and found we were to be flying with Pilot/Officer Jim Heflin #1983. We departed Phoenix around 5 PM flying southeast towards New Mexico. We were armed with our issued sidearms. I was sitting right seat next to Jim at the controls, Charlie was in the rear, trying to plan our portion of the activities that would take place later.

As we neared New Mexico, Jim told me we were going to try to get clearance to fly through military air operation areas to expedite our travel time. Otherwise we would have to skirt those areas leading to at least an hour or two more of flight time. I have a headset on, so I am monitoring Jim's conversation with Air Traffic Control when he asked for a direct heading to Brownsville. The controller in Albuquerque Center asked if we were Oxxxx(a US Customs call sign) and Jim replied no, but we were a State of Arizona law enforcement aircraft. The controller came back shortly and told us he saw on his log who we were and cleared us direct to Brownsville. Later he called as we were going into another air traffic control center and told Jim ours was the first nonfederal aircraft that had been cleared to fly through that area in his years of working that center.

We landed in Brownsville about 9:30 pm and were met by Texas DPS and taken to a motel where we were briefed on what had been going on since last talking to them in the afternoon. Jim elected to stay at the motel as he had been flying all day and wanted to be ready to go once the bust was going to occur.

Charlie and I stuck with Ray Coffman and George Olivo the rest of the night and early in the morning, the load crew started moving around and were surveilled as they went down to the Rio Grande, met with other Colombians and transferred the load into rubber rafts and brought the load across into the United States. They loaded the duffle bags into a vehicle and brought them to the stash house that Texas had been watching closely for several days. Once inside, they did a few things and then departed the stash house in two separate vehicles. Charlie and I stayed with Ray Coffman and the surveillance team lost sight of one of the cars , but as luck would have it, that vehicle passed right in front of us. Coffman decided to stop the vehicle before we lost it again, so now Charlie and I, two Narcs from Arizona are in the middle of the road in Brownsville, Texas, roughly 1300 air miles from home, in a location where neither of us had ever been, where we didn't know where we were, in our normal street clothes, shirts, Wranglers and boots, Arizona DPS badges on our belts, holding several people at gunpoint, alongside a Texas DPS Narcotics officer that we had only met in person a few hours before.

The bust resulted in the largest cocaine seizure in Texas at that time, a Beech Queen Air plane, a couple of pickup truck, two rubber rafts and about $10,000 in cash, several arrests, all the direct result of some excellent police work over several months in Arizona by Charlie Ruiz and the Air Interdiction Unit, and great cooperation by the Texas DPS and U.S. Customs officers in Brownsville, Texas and quick work by our bosses at DPS and U.S. Customs in Phoenix to make our involvement in Brownsville happen.

And, unfortunately, Jim Heflin slept through it! He still hasn't forgiven us for not waking him up in time, but as they say south of the border, "Asi es la vida!

Cleared Direct to Brownsville

Jim Heflin #1983

I remember returning to the DPS hangar late afternoon in the Beechcraft Baron after a day of flying that started early that morning. Upon my arrival, Chief Pilot John McKean #217 advised me to go home get a change of clothes, that I would be flying Officer Charlie Ruiz #1267 and Sergeant Colin Peabody #481 to Brownsville, Texas.

I told John if time is of the essence, we need to take the King Air (#911AZ) because we could not do a non-stop flight without refueling in the Baron due to having to fly around the restricted US Military Air Operations areas. John still advised that I would be taking the Baron.

Upon my return to the DPS hangar, I was surprised to see the King Air assigned and ready to go. John didn't seem to be happy. John told me that Col. Forgia #92 called him and told him to schedule the King Air for the Texas trip. I can't prove it, but I wouldn't be surprised if Lt. Reutter #621 stirred things up the chain to get the aircraft changed. Just before departure, John told me to ask for direct routing through the military operations areas, the big ask being through the White Sands Proving Grounds.

We departed at approximately 1700 hours. About 1 hour later we were handed off to the Albuquerque Center controller, who controlled the White Sands airspace. With little confidence, I requested direct routing to Brownsville. The controller asked if we were Oxxxx, a U.S. Customs call sign. I replied negative, but we were a state law enforcement aircraft. There was a pause then the controller replied "OK, I see now. King Air 1 Alpha Zulu, cleared direct to Brownsville." When we were about to be handed off to the next sector, the controller came on the air and said "1 Alpha Zulu, in all my years at Albuquerque

Center, you are the first non-U.S. Government aircraft to be cleared through this airspace.

I thought then, thanks to U.S. Customs and my sometimes hard headed boss to call ahead for this trip. During my later airline career I flew this routing several times and never got the special clearance we got that evening. We arrived in Brownsville about 9:30 local time. I chose to get a motel room so I would be rested for the big bust. The next thing I recall was a Brownsville Police Officer was sent to pick me up. When I arrived at the PD, I found out that I had missed the takedown! Oh Well, at least I got in on the group photo of everybody involved in this operation.

From the biography of Texas Ranger Lt. Ray Coffman

Reproduced with the permission of the Texas Rangers Hall of Fame and Museum.

In 1982, Florida law enforcement agencies were making things so hot for South American drug smugglers that they decided to try a new route. The Arizona State Police had a well-placed informant within the cartel who told the Arizona officials that a Colombian drug cartel was considering a test run from Columbia through Mexico and crossing into the United States at Brownsville. Brownsville was in Ray's area, and it

was at this point that Arizona officials contacted him.
Ray had been furnished the name and phone number of the informant by the Arizona officials. Ray contacted him and found out that the drug movement was not only on "go," but was scheduled to cross into Texas within the week.
At the time, Ray had four narcotic investigators and two task force troopers (Highway Patrolmen) in his command. All of this force was involved in drug investigations, and the only man Ray could pull away to assist him was Sergeant George Olivo. Later, Trooper Steve Vestal was able to join them.
For the next four days and nights, Olivo, Ray, and later Vestal conducted surveillance on a known stash house in Brownsville. During the early morning hours of the fifth morning, things started happening.
Vestal, dressed in camos (camouflage clothing), was across the road in some bushes near the stash house. Olivo and Ray manned mobile units about a block on each side of the house. Vestal saw the garage door open, and six people, dressed in camos, got into a pickup containing two inflatable rafts.
When the truck left, Olivo and Ray followed. Olivo and Ray followed the truck until it stopped near the mouth of the Rio Grande River at the Gulf of Mexico. The occupants unloaded the rafts and

crossed the river. For about an hour, they met with some Columbians, who gave them seven duffel bags. They then loaded their new cargo into the rafts, re-crossed the Rio Grande, loaded the bags into the truck, and left. Ray and Olivo followed the Columbians back to the stash house and observed them unloading the duffel bags.
For several hours, Olivo and Ray sat and waited. Just before daylight, things started happening. The stash house's garage door opened and two vehicles drove out in opposite directions. A car carried four people, two Columbian men and two women. A pickup contained two Columbian men. Olivo pursued the car, and Ray took off after the pickup. After short chases, the Rangers apprehended both vehicles. At the time this was the largest cocaine seizure in Texas history and the second largest in U.S. history with seized property consisting of numerous weapons and 350 lbs. of drugs valued at $2.8 million.

What's A Few Dollars Between Brothers?

John Fink #683

While working at DPS I had two brothers who were also on the force - Marty Fink and Richard Fink.
There was another Fink also whose name was Skip. Skip was one of a kind. Many times DPS would get our checks mixed up and he would receive my check which was more than his and

easily recognizable but good old Skip rather than notifying payroll would simply cash it and then pay it back later. Me, on the other hand, I would notify payroll and then have to wait for them to send me a corrected check. Hey, who could blame him. That meant he didn't have to wait on his money!

I would give him a hard time about this and he would always say what's a few dollars between brothers. I would always remind him that we weren't brothers but he would joke around and always insist that we were!

Now that Skip is no longer with us, I am going to have to admit that we are in fact Brothers and will always be. I miss you Skip and hope one day us "Brothers" will be together again!

Eloy

Harley Thompson #6

In the late summer of 1949 the saga of Eloy reared its ugly head.

I was stationed in Winslow at that time and one afternoon during the late summer I received a phone call from Assistant Superintendent Jack Powell asking me to come to Phoenix for a special assignment.

"If I may ask Chief, just where is this assignment and for how long, so I may come equipped" I asked. "Eloy" he said, "and the time line is indefinite. We don't know how long it will take."

Eloy, at that time, from all I had heard and read was the Tombstone of the day. Bodies were piling up in the morgue at an alarming rate.

"Just what is it you want me to do down there" I asked. "Just come on down in the morning to headquarters and be there about noon and Superintendent Walker will explain in detail what he has in mind". "Yes sir" I said. "I'll be there."

It was about 0 dark 30 in the morning when I high tailed it out of Winslow and headed for Phoenix. During the trip down I had a long time to think, and I truly wondered what in the Sam Hill am I getting into this time. I had read the papers about problems that were occurring down there and I knew this was not a friendly place for police officers or anyone else representing any law enforcement organization. I felt sorta like a one legged chicken going into a den of hungry coyotes. Well, I thought, Superintendent A.G. Walker will lay it all out I'm sure.

Sometime after the lunch hour Superintendent Walker called me into his office. Present at the time was Assistant Superintendent Powell, Inspector Bryan and Captain Murphy. Chief Walker asked me if I was aware of the situation in Eloy and the surrounding communities in Pinal County. I told he I knew only what I had heard and read in the newspapers. He told me at that time that my going down there would be voluntary and that I could simply return to Winslow and they would find someone else. (I knew then, by what he said, that Jack Powell had assured him that I would accept this special assignment.) I told Chief Walker that I fully understood and that I was more than willing to do whatever he desired.

Chief Walker told me that I would be living with the family of Patrolman Bert Babb. He further stated that this had all be cleared with Babb and his family. He also said that I would be on full expenses for the entire duration of my stay down there and that I would sign over my expense checks to the family to compensate them for room and board. He told me that I would also see the chief clerk before I left and that I would be issued a Thompson sub-machine gun and several extra magazines and ammunition for the weapon. Chief Walker went on to say that my primary job would be that of keeping Patrolman Babb alive. There had been several attempts on his life, the windshield of his patrol vehicle had been shot out and he had received numerous threats against his life. Chief Walker said that I was to carry the machine gun with me constantly and that included going into restaurants, coffee shops and elsewhere, that I was to make my presence known all over town and anyplace else we happened to go at any time and I was never to leave Patrolman Babb alone at any time, except at night when we were in his home. He told me to go on down there that day, as they were expecting me and that in about 5 or 6 days we would be summoned back up to headquarters where we would attend a meeting with a large number of people and that at that time a plan of action would be outlined for the next few weeks or months as may be required.

I high tailed it on down to Eloy that afternoon and spent the next 3 or 4 days getting acquainted with Patrolman Babb, his family, and the area in and around Pinal County. I was also vitally interested in who were the "Kingpins" in the drug, gambling and houses of ill repute. Patrolman Babb filled me in on all the information I had requested. Five days later we received orders to come to headquarters in Phoenix, to go by Casa Grande, pick up Patrolman Bud Kratzberg and be in the office by 1000 hours. The superintendent had everyone go across the hall to the Highway Department meeting room since Chief Walker's office was much too small to accommodate all those who would be in attendance. When we finally all gathered, those present were Superintendent Walker, Assistant Superintendent Jack Powell, Inspector Riley Byran, Captain Dysart Murphy, Patrolman Babb, Kratzberg and myself from the highway patrol, the sheriff from Pinal County, Assistant Attorney General Perry Ling representing the state of Arizona, and two suits from the federal government, one of which was the SAC of the FBI and the other from the Bureau of Internal Revenue. There was another suit who came to the meeting just after chief Walker called us to order, and whoever he was, he was not introduced.

Chief Walker didn't mince any words. He started off by addressing his remarks to the Pinal County sheriff. Calling the sheriff by name, he said, "you and I have been friends for many years, we both grew up together in Pinal County. I'm an old man and have not been well for some time and it won't be long before I have to leave this job and retire. But before I do, I'm going to see to it that Pinal County is cleaned up, the gambling, drugs and all the whores and other trash is removed." He went on to say, "Sheriff, your chief deputy is on the take with some of the gambling operations and the first thing you're going to do when you get back this afternoon is to fire the man." He went on to say that he would come down to Pinal County with the Highway Patrol and clean it up for him if he didn't start taking some action. At this point the sheriff started blustering and denying that his deputies weren't working and he told Chief Walker that he didn't have the authority to enforce any laws except on the highways. It was then that Mr. Ling of the attorney general's office took over and laid it out in very plain English for the sheriff stating that the highway patrol had the authority to not only enforce the laws of the state relating to the highways but elsewhere throughout the state as well. Mr. Ling said, "In other words sheriff, they have the authority of state police. The only limitations they have would be Indian reservations, military bases and other federal properties."

The old sheriff grumbled a bit more and he promised Chief Walker that he would help him. There was a lot of reluctance in his statement. They all talked a bit more and then the sheriff left the meeting. The federal boys said they had several "undercover" men working in Eloy and a couple of other places in Pinal County. They went on to say that their operatives would meet with Patrolman Kratzberg, Babb and myself the next Sunday night at the home of Patrolman Kratzberg in Casa Grande at 2300 hours. The purpose of this meeting would be for us to be able to identify their personnel. They went on to say that in the event we should at any time see their operatives or come into contact that we were not to indicate any recognition whatsoever. The meeting adjourned and Chief Walker turned to us and said, "Boys, I want this to all be over just as soon as possible. Do what you have to do."

On Sunday we met with the federal people. They gave us some photos of a number of individuals that they had under surveillance together with names and places of employment and businesses they were associated with in the county. They also named the same guy that Babb had named as the one having the most active involvement in gambling, whores, drugs and other illegal activities. (To this day I do not remember the name of this guy, so for purposes of this story I shall call him exactly what he was. Slime Ball). The federal guys also said that we would have a meeting at

Kratzberg's house once a month on the last Sunday and at the same time for comparing notes, etc.

Babb and I worked some very irregular hours for the next 3 weeks or so and we did this in order to confuse locals about our having an established work pattern. We even went into a number of bars and went into the back rooms and broke up both poker and crap games and in every case we left word that we were looking for "Slime Ball", even though we knew he was not around. What we were trying to do was push Slime Ball into making a move toward us or making some other mistake which would give us reason to bust him for some felony action. We were trying to "tick him off something fierce". One night while on patrol we stopped one of the buses he owned which transported farm workers to the fields and brought them back to the shacks where they lived. This particular bus had a tail light out and the driver complained that it was only one of the two tail lights and that this was OK. In no uncertain terms, I told him that was not the case. My tone of voice and the presence of the machine gun told him I was correct! He said, "Slime Ball will hear about this and you will be sorry you ever came to Pinal County." I told him, "Good we are looking for that crook anyway. Be damned sure you do."

Every weekend additional highway patrolmen would come into the Pinal County area. With the weekend influx of these patrolmen there were many good drug bust made, as we continued to put pressure on all areas of illegal activities.

The more legitimate businessmen of Eloy for some time had been working very hard to have the community incorporate and become a city. This became a reality, I believe it was November of 1949, and began organizing a police department and other necessary functions of city government.

At the next meeting we had at the end of the month in Casa Grande, the Feds told us that the pressure we were applying was beginning to have a great effect on old Slime Ball and some of his henchmen. The way one of them put it was, "They're beginning to act like a bunch of long tailed cats in a room full of rocking chairs. They're getting real nervous." They suggested we continue our efforts and push real hard in the hopes that some way or another the "Bad Guys" would try something foolish and we could bring this situation to a close. We suggested to the undercover guys, if you can let us know when Slime Ball is going to be out of town and we'll get the deputies to help us break up a few card games, make a couple of seizures of his worker buses for equipment failures, and leave some hard words to the effect that we are damned unhappy about some of his crap and that we are looking for him. In order for this to be effective, we have to know he is really out of town.

A week or so went by and early one day Patrolman Babb found a note stuck under his windshield wiper blade. The note stated that old Slime Ball was going to California for a few days. Knowing this, we made contact with a couple of Pinal County deputies and included them in our plans. They agreed to help us, so we went to work and started closing down some of his operations in the back rooms of the bars. The deputies made a few arrests and we left some extremely harsh words about wanting to find Slime Ball and "end his reign of crime". We also grounded a couple of buses for equipment failures,, stating that they were unsafe and by utilizing an old section of the motor vehicle code and a seizure book that I had, we had the vehicles towed off to the nearest Highway Department yard. (At one time during the 1940's all highway patrolmen had a seizure book, much like a citation or warning book, and under the old 66 series code, we could legally seize motor vehicles and take them off the road). In this case it was a great asset.

At the last meet we had with the Feds, they informed us that they had enough evidence to take old Slime Ball down for income tax evasion and some interstate transportation of his whores he had taken back and forth to California and gave us a phone number to use in the event it looked like he would run.

The following weekend Superintendent Walker sent about a half dozen more units to Pinal County. These were in addition to the usual weekend units and working with some of the younger dedicated

Pinal County deputies, we really cracked down hard on the entire area.
After our enforcement actions and the investigations by the Feds, the feds made their arrest and charged him with several offenses. During the next few days the gambling games were gone and the whore houses closed and a sort of calm prevailed in the county. Eloy in the meantime had their police department up and running. They hired a retired Washington. D.C. officer as the chief. His name was Haggerty, I believe, and we began relaxing somewhat.
It was now December and there were many changes up north along US66. Patrolmen Whitlow, Cochran, Raymond and Stinson had all been promoted to the rank of captain. I received a call from headquarters from Assistant Superintendent Jack Powell to come up to Phoenix as my assignment in Eloy was over. Upon arriving in Phoenix, Chief Walker thanked me for my efforts and informed me that I was to now report for duty in Holbrook. Another choice assignment????????

A Hard Landing

Ben Hancock #2676

When I was a young patrolman working in D6, part of my beat was the Coolidge/Florence/Eloy area. There was an old USAF training airport there and they were flying T-37s from Williams AFB into there for pattern work with student pilots. It

was always a very popular parachute jump center also (even Navy Seals have used it).
I was always stopping these hippie jumpers near there for speeding and such and they kept inviting me to jump with them. So I decided to give it a try. My Sergeant, Marshall Goade, told me I would be an idiot to jump with those potheads. They did give me a big discount. I spent a Saturday morning in jump school there and then they gave me a chute and a reserve, and I climbed into a modified Cessna with no seats with 4 other new jumpers. Two of them were big German tourists who looked like SS Stormtroopers and were wearing black military style jumpsuits. After we climbed up with each lap around the airfield they would send one student out the door to jump. It was a static line jump using the classic big ole military chutes. I was the last one out and I figured if any of the other 4 had any problems I wasn't going to jump. My turn came and out I went. I counted to 5, got a big opening shock and looked up to check my chute and instead of the big green one that everyone else had I had a smaller orange and white reserve chute. They told me afterwards that they ran out of packed regular chutes and because I was pretty light, they gave me a reserve for my main. But they "forgot" to tell me. But I remembered them telling us that if you used the reserve you would come down faster and harder. Damn it. So I spent so much time thinking about that and the upcoming hard landing and the fact that the wind

was obviously going to push me out of the dirt drop area and it was soon apparent that I was going to land on an asphalt runway. I failed to turn into the wind and did a downwind landing on the asphalt. I busted the heck out of my right rear butt cheek and hip (nothing broken). I couldn't even sit upright for days after that. Sgt Goade was right! But I did not want that to be my last experience so weeks later I went back out and had the hippie jump master guarantee me a main chute or I was going to arrest his ass for possession or something. The second jump was textbook. I was going to jump again when a PCSO Deputy called me out there one day to see the results of a fatal jump. An Air Force student pilot who had jumped competitively at the USAFA was sport jumping with some of his buddies and had a main chute malfunction. He tried to fix it and then was late to cut it loose and pull his reserve and he hit the ground with a partial chute. DRT. Dead right there. He was doing what I wanted to do - fly military jets and there he was dead in the dirt in Pinal County near the small towns of Coolidge, Florence and Eloy. I never jumped again. I prayed a lot in the Harrier jet but never had to pull the ejection seat handle.

Patrol Car For Sale

Louie Chaboya #1139

Captain Jaime Teyechea #44 (May he rest in Peace) and Sergeant John Davis #146 would often park a patrol car in front of the office close to the road as a deterrent so people would think that an officer was watching for any traffic violations. One day Captain Teyechea was in his office when a gentleman from Nogales, Sonora walked into his office asking how much the patrol car was selling for. Captain Teyechea advised the gentleman that the patrol car was not for sale. The gentleman then asked Captain Teyechea why was a sign that said "SE VENDE" (For Sale in Spanish) on the patrol car? YEP, George Rider had placed the sign on the patrol car.

Ma'am I Hate To Tell You

Dick Lewis #176

The following is something I wrote that appeared as a guest editorial in the Glendale newspaper on July 15, 1970.

This is not a shooting war, there aren't even two sides. This war is comprised of only one army. The American motoring public. This army is making war upon itself.

There are many people who have driven cars for many years and have never had an accident. They may continue to do so. On the other hand, there are many who have lived through serious accidents only to be involved in other serious accidents.

Then there are the many unfortunate ones who have had or were involved in just one accident. This was their first and last.

The sad part of this is that many of them had never driven an automobile; they weren't old enough.

As I stop a violator who is driving at a high speed, and he protests as I am writing out the citation, I wonder if he has ever seen any of the carnage that this machine has caused. Has he ever seen a human who was slaughtered by this kind of conduct. I think that he has not.

As I stop a happy motorist who stands weaving before me, shaking his finger and blowing his sickening alcohol saturated breath in my face, I know that he is ignorant to what he has to lose. He protests that he has to answer to the law that was created to protect the public from just this sort of offense.

I am considered this man's personal enemy. Actually, I am just a scape goat at which he can vent his wrath. I understand, and he does not. He is his own enemy.

I am considered public enemy number one among motorists. When I am not around, they do what they want, and then suffer the consequences.

What really hurts, and what I shall never get used to, are the personal heartbreaks involved.

To extract a broken body from a hulk of twisted steel, is a matter of routine. There are facts to gather, an investigation to complete.

At the scene of the accident, it is a nightmare. The smell of gasoline and oil, bright lights flashing, people wanting to help and not knowing what to do make it complete.

A child cried out from the darkness, "I hurt". I find him, both arms are broken.

A service man is semiconscious and inquires about his buddy. His buddy lies decapitated where he was thrown before the car came to a rest. It had rolled three times.

Only after the last victim has been removed from the scene, and the last measurement has been taken, does the full impact of what has happened fall around my shoulders. There is only one more detail to take care of, to notify the next of kin.

The dread knock on the door in the dead of night. A mother starts to the door still tying her house coat. Out back of the house a dog barks. I know that when this door opens and she sees me standing there, she expects the worse.

When the door opens this mother's world will never be the same again. Her world of peace and security will be shattered, and she will be burdened with grief and despair.

It is agony to tell the loved one of another that her son, daughter or husband has been killed.

I hear only one small, indescribable cry, a shrill sob, the sound of a small hurt animal. It tears the soul from your body in sympathy.

I wish I could bring back that person's loved one, to recreate what has been destroyed. It is impossible, so I offer my assistance and make sure she is looked after in her disbelieving grief. Then I leave feeling small and guilty.

I have knocked on these doors and spoken these cruel words, "Ma'am, your son was in an accident this evening and was killed". There is no other way to say it.

I write these words with a hollow feeling in my stomach. I know for certain that I shall have to say them over and over and over again.

As a parting word to the drinking driver, the sleepy tourist, and the carefree teenager, I quote a passage of the last rites, "Lord, we return them from where they came, ashes to ashes and dust to dust.

Deadman's Curve

Richard Richardson #188

As a rookie during the three months of the summer of 1962, I patrolled the Yuma area of District 4. It was very busy time for me: my first written traffic ticket (citation), first DUI arrest, first Dyer Act (Stolen vehicle from out of state), high speed pursuit chases, and all three classifications of traffic accidents: Codes 961 (property), 962 (injury) and 963 (fatality).

The first fatality really stuck in my mind. Highway 95, between Yuma and San Luis (on the Mexico border) was well known death trap for drunk drivers coming up from a day's partying at Mexican bars. One night I received a radio dispatch about an accident at 'Dead Man's Curve'. Highway 95 was basically a fairly straight road, except for two full 90 degree turns close together. Northbound drivers under the influence tend to not see the curves at times and, well, not make one of the turns. And . . . Viola! . . . There's a crash.

I was the first officer to arrive at the scene of such a crash. It is known that the first officer arriving at a crash scene is the investigating officer and other officers arrive are assisting in the investigation. Patrolmen didn't have cameras in those days. A sergeant is called out on all fatality and most serious injury accidents to take photos of the scene. Sergeant Chick Lawwill #717 arrived at the scene. The crash involved one vehicle, missing the infamous Dead Man's curve. A Volkswagen had rolled more than once, and some occupants were ejected. One of the passengers was a US Marine, who was celebrating his marriage. He and his new bride were in the back seat when the accident occurred. The others in the vehicle were seriously injured. The dispatcher was advised that a Marine was involved. The Marine Air Station in Yuma was advised and sent a representative to the scene. This procedure isn't usually done, except the deceased was a Marine in uniform and I believed that the base should be notified.

This was such a waste of human life because of improper alcohol use and inattention of the driver. One of the other officers at the scene did make a DUI arrest of an individual that happened to stop at the scene.

A Mission of Mercy Blood Run

Colin Peabody #481

In November 1968, I was working the late shift and I responded to a call for assistance from the Winslow PD for a medical emergency at the Duke City Lumber Company located on the south side of Winslow. This lumber company processed the Ponderosa Pine timber that was cut down on the Mogollon Rim several miles south of Winslow and trucked to the mill. When I got there I found that two workers had gotten caught in the de-barking machine and were seriously injured. The de-barking machine stripped the bark off the logs that were loaded onto a conveyor belt and as the logs went through the machine, all the bark was stripped off before the logs went for further milling.

We were able to extract the two workers, who lost much of their clothing, but lost a lot of the flesh from their lower legs, exposing their leg bones, a gruesome sight for anyone, let alone this young, rookie Highway Patrolman. The two men were transported to the Winslow Hospital a couple of miles away and treated as quickly as possible. Their injuries were severe and they had both lost a lot of blood. The hospital called Phoenix for additional blood supplies. There were no commercial aircraft flying into Winslow at that time of the night, but the blood was needed sooner than the next available flight which would have been the next day. This was before DPS had their helicopters in service.

A call was made to AHP headquarters to see if blood could be transported from Phoenix to Winslow and the Patrol okayed that transport. A Phoenix patrolman was to pick up the blood and start north. A problem cropped up in that no units north of Phoenix were available and Flagstaff had no units available either. I was working and the decision was made for me to meet the Phoenix unit at a midway point somewhere around the area north of Camp Verde and I would bring the blood into Winslow from there. So at about midnight, I headed for Flagstaff 60+ miles away and quickly gassed up at a Chevron station there before heading south to meet the other patrolman. We met around the Sedona exit and I headed north with at least 100 miles of Code 3 driving ahead of me. There was still construction on what would be I-17 and I-40 wasn't completed through Flagstaff or east of Flag, so it was a two lane highway most of the way north and east on U.S. Route 66. As I went through Flagstaff, the road was somewhat icy and when I went through the railroad underpass in downtown Flag, my car was sideways, but I was able to recover and continue on. Once out of Flagstaff, the trip went quicker and we got the blood safely delivered to the hospital. That night, two Arizona Highway Patrolmen went on a several hundred mile mission of mercy to help save the lives of two critically injured men, who eventually recovered months later.

Proud To Serve

Dick Lewis #176

The night is very dark. It is raining and has been for several hours. This is a tense time of year. The time of our summer storms.

I am standing in the middle of the road. It is a downgrade to the north and there is a blind curve to the south.

The flares light up the roadway and reflect a red ball against the wet black surface of the road. I am holding one in my hand to flag traffic.

Over the bank on the east side of the road, a pickup is on its top in a group of large boulders. I can't help but think how awkward and unnatural it looks.

Lying in different locations around the vehicle are victims of this accident. They are being attended to by my partner and other motorists who have stopped to help. The victims aren't too badly injured, if it is correct to say, not critical. Just the same, they are injured and are getting wet. I can see several persons holding a tarp over a man to keep off the rain.

The ambulance is taking a long time to arrive. I understand this. The road is washed out in several places and there are rocks on the highway and slick spots. He must be careful also.

I continue to direct traffic around the scene. I have to keep it moving to avoid another accident.

I patiently coax the cautious around, speed up the curious and politely thank the offers of assistance.

Most everyone cooperates in an emergency such as this. Any equipment that we may need in this particular situation is provided. If it is not available here, it is obtained and brought to us.

The ambulance has arrived now and the injured are being lifted gently under the supervision of the other patrolman, and are placed on the stretcher. The ambulance now departs.

The wrecker and its able crew arrive and survey the situation. The patrolman in charge gives them the nod, "O K boys we can move it now." The crew wheel the machinery into position and swing into action.

The investigating officer leaves to do follow-up at the hospital.

I am still in charge of the traffic flow and the clean-up operation. It doesn't take long, however. The wrecker crew is good. They and the ambulance driver, like myself have been to the scene of many mishaps.

Now everyone is gone and there is a sudden stillness I realize. The flares are burned out, leaving the night even darker.

I start down the hill and the road crews are working on the washouts. They are blading the rocks out of the roadway and sanding the slick spots. A light rain still falls.

I see the lights of town now below me shining brightly. It is comforting to know that there are people in this town. People, who in the time of need and emergency will come to help.

Later in the evening I learn that the victims of this accident are in satisfactory condition.

I think back on the events of the evening. There were many citizens there helping. I wish I could pin a medal on each of them. I can only offer my "Thank you sir" in an attempt to show my appreciation.

This is only one of the countless instances which have occurred where people have assisted us. This is only one of the many instances which makes me proud to serve the motoring public on the highways and the wonderful people of this great state of Arizona.

A True Hero

Ron Bruce #2048

On September 11th, 1994, I was working traffic on US 89 at milepost 445, around 1845 hours. I checked a northbound black Chevrolet Suburban at 67 MPH on my radar and could see that the driver was not wearing a seat belt. I was again patrolling in my 1992 Camaro. Stopping that vehicle, I approached on the passenger side, identified myself and asked the driver for his license, registration and proof of insurance. He had a cowboy hat on but seemed very familiar. Looking at his Arizona driver's license when his wife handed it out her window, I then quickly realized I was standing in the presence of one of my childhood heroes, USMC Medal of Honor winner, Joe Foss.

During WWII Gen. Foss was the leading USMC aviator fighter pilot during the Battle of Guadalcanal, having shot down 26 Japanese aircraft. There was absolutely no way I could convince myself to issue him a citation, the only time I ever felt that way. I issued him a written warning (I still have the original copy) for 64+ and the seat belt use. When I was done with the contact I visited more with him and his wife, Donna Wild Foss. I learned they were on their way to Lander, WY for the annual "One Shot Antelope Hunt".

As I was wrapping up the contact, Gen. Foss said he had something for me and to continue to visit with Donna. I told the General that it was against policy to accept anything from a violator. He responded that I had done my job as I saw fit, that he appreciated that but I was going to have to humor him. He was at the back of the Suburban for a couple of minutes and returned to my side of the Chevy. He handed me a copy of his hardbound autobiography, "A Proud American". It had been inscribed as follows, "My best wishes to Officer Ron Bruce, God Bless You! Joe Foss, 11SEPT'94". I was speechless and that book and the original warning remain some of my treasured possessions and memories.

About one year later, I was attending a gun show at the Fairgrounds in Phoenix. As I perused the treasures therein, I spotted what was now something of a familiar figure walking down that aisle towards me. Lo and behold if it wasn't Gen. Foss! He had a significant entourage trailing behind him. I had no intention other than to say hello as he passed by me. However, as he neared, he slowed and came to a stop in front of me. He said, "Well I'll be darned if it isn't Trooper Bruce!" I was stunned that he would recognize me in that setting and looking significantly different than I did that 1994 September evening. I commented on that and the General responded that he had been blessed at remembering faces and names. We chatted for perhaps five minutes. He said, "Well, guess I'd best be moving on. Some of these folks with me are getting antsy." That was my last ever contact with Joe Foss but, even in death, like my Father, he remains one of my heroes.

(Note) Besides being a Medal Of Honor recipient and holding the rank of General, he was also South Dakota Governor, president of the National Rifle Association and first commissioner of the American Football League.
A great Man!

Your Ride Is On The Way

Paul Palmer #342

It was in the mid 70's and I was working the sergeants desk in Phoenix Op Comm when a dispatcher told me she kept getting calls from a drunk down in Coolidge demanding a ride from DPS.
She asked me to talk to the guy. When the phone rang again, I answered it and sure enough it was the drunk. He said that he was in a phone booth in front of a bar and needed a ride to the Coolidge LARK center.
I advised him that we could not help him. He began the usual tirade we have heard so much. I pay taxes. You work for me. What's your badge number? I'll have your job. I told him he might call the Coolidge police department or the sheriff's office.
He was still ranting when I hung up the phone.

The phone rang again. Same drunk. We went through the same routine. The phone rang again. Same drunk wanting a ride from DPS. The guy must have had a pocket full of change.

When he called the fourth time, I was getting kind of tired of this guy. After telling him over and over that we would not provide him with a ride he said, "What if I told you I was going to kill the president?" I said, "That will probably work."

I then got the phone number he was calling from and the name of the bar. I told him someone would be there to get him. Then I called the Phoenix FBI office. I gave the agent all the information about the threat. He thanked me and we were free of the drunk's calls for the remainder of the shift. I typed up the information on the log and forgot about it as I headed home after the shift.

Later that morning as I was sleeping my wife woke me up and said an FBI agent was on the phone for me. The agent asked me about the calls and asked if I had any more information. I told him that no, he had all the information. He then told me that they had the guy at the Pinal County sheriff's office and thanked me for my help.

Guess he got his ride after all.

Patrolman Dick Shafer investigates an accident in 1956

Sgt Jim Eaves and officer Jim Oyen watch as Officer Frank Gonzales administers a field sobriety test

Highway Patrolman administers first aid to an accident victim in 1954

Lt Bob Broan on left and an unidentified Lt at a traffic safety presentation year unknown

L-R Holbrook Dispatchers Pat McCollum, Robin Haskel, Lena Barret, Paul Short, Sgt Hickman 1964

Naco School members of the Arizona Highway Patrol School Safety Patrol 1951

L-R Officers Charlie Ruiz, AZDPS, George Olivos Texas DPS, Jim Heflin, AZDPS, Colin Peabody AZDPS, Agent Ray Coffman Texas DPS. The Mexican Connection Brownsville, Texas Feb. 1984

Officers from Utah, New Mexico, Arizona and Colorado meet at Four Corners for a special enforcement detail

Patrolman Dick Lewis and Miami PD officer along with citizens carry a body out of the canyon at Bloody Tanks on US60. The fatality occurred in 1963

Patrolmen investigate a fatality east of Perryville in 1951

Lt Bert Zambonini and Capt Pat McCollum inspect
Class #10 cadets 1968

DPS Headquarters 1980's

Sgt John Gantt Sr in riot gear 1967

DPS Air Rescue helicopter

Bomb dropped on Iraq during First Gulf War by USMC Harrier pilot Lt Kevin Gross

Husband and wife team. Cindy and Lee Patterson

AHP/DPS Heritage Museum, Phoenix Headquarters

Former Director Col. Silbert at the Brick Reveal Jan. 2023

Lt Bob Broan and comedian Jerry Lewis on a movie set in Kingman

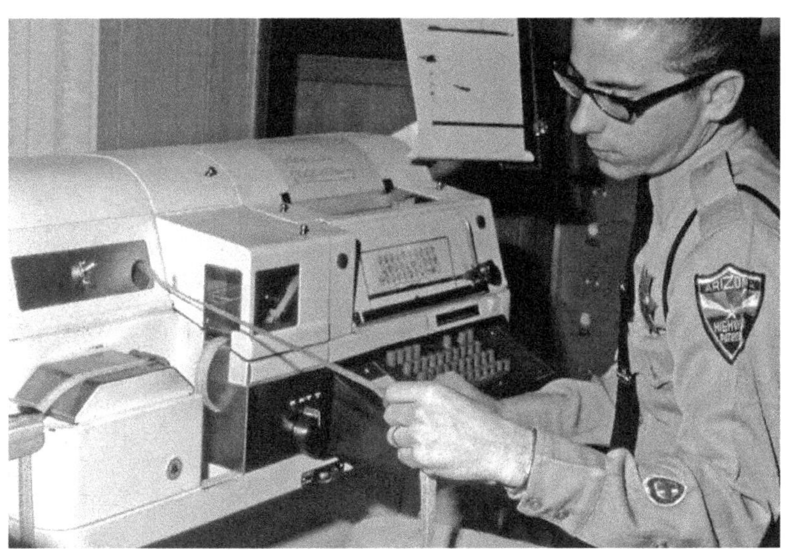

Patrolman Paul Palmer relaying NLETS traffic in Phoenix Communications 1969

Interior of 1962 Ford patrol car with under the dash A/C and retro police speedometer

Officer Bob Stein during Traffic Safety PSA taping in San Diego Harbor 1991

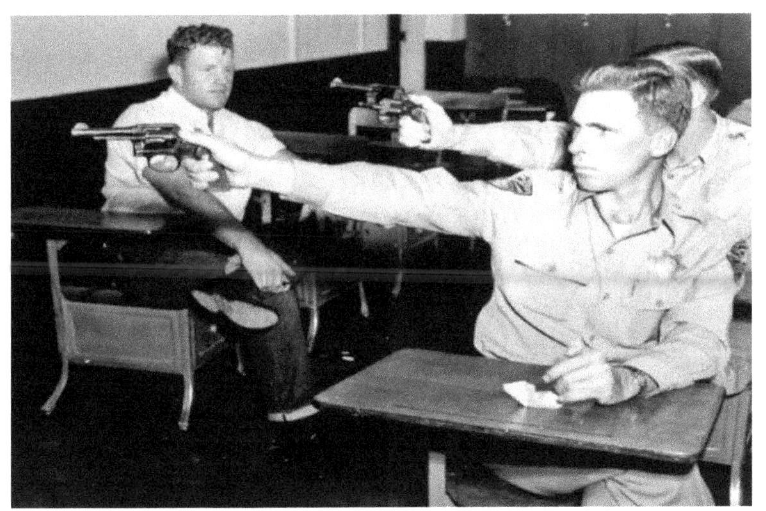

Patrolman Dick Raymond during firearms training

Officer Bob Stein and NASCAR great Richard Petty at taping of a Traffic Safety PSA at Phoenix International Raceway

Where's The Cow?

Darryl Mullins #480

It was in the early 1970's, I was working an evening shift in the old Dist. 5 on I-17 in Phoenix. I had just exited the freeway N-bound at Camelback. It was during the Rodeo Days at the Fairgrounds when dispatch made a general broadcast advising a steer was missing and feared gotten out of the rodeo grounds. Dispatch advised all units to be on the lookout for the steer.

I was pulling up to the intersection of Camelback and the I-17 frontage road. I looked past the intersection and saw a steer that was heading for the n-bound freeway on-ramp. I was able to head the steer away from the ramp, so it continued north on the frontage road. I called it in to dispatch and they advised they would contact the Livestock Inspector.

The steer went into neighborhoods with patrol cars and Phoenix marked units joining in. The steer was going over front yards when a P.D. unit decided to cut it off by pulling into a driveway. The steer just stopped and went around the P.D. unit at a slow trot. In the meantime there was a patrolman that was trying to find us to join in. It was a fluid situation and we were traveling through many neighborhoods. The steer finally came out at the old Christown Mall. It was later in the evening so the mall was closed and the parking lot was empty. This whole time the one patrolman kept asking where we were.

The Livestock Inspector caught up with us at the mall parking lot. He got his lasso out and got on the hood of a P.D. unit. The P.D.unit took the lead and he tried to lasso the steer a couple of times with no luck. At one point the steer was trotting alongside a neighbor's wooden fence when a P.D.unit tried to cut the steer off and took out about 10 ft. of the wooden fence. The steer stopped, backed up and went around the P.D. unit. The whole time the one patrolman kept asking where we were. The Livestock Inspector got into position again the third time was the charm. He lassoed the steer about the time the one patrolman found us. He motioned for the patrolman to pull up to where he was. The inspector tied the steer onto the patrolman push bumper. The rodeo people were called and were sending out a cattle trailer. We all left and the one patrolman was stuck with the steer tied to his bumper.

I didn't mention the ONE PATROLMAN'S name because he was a good patrolman and a great guy that just had a bit of bad luck.

Do You Know Where The Jail Is?

Bob Ticer #4490

Back in the early 90's when I was a patrolman out of the Cordes Junction squad, our Northern

Division Commander put out a directive that he wanted a graveyard car on I-17 between the Phoenix city limits and the Coconino County line, north of Stoneman Lake. The shift would rotate monthly between the Black Canyon City, Cordes Junction, and Camp Verde squads between 2200 hours and 0600 hours. Most of the old timers didn't want to work this shift, so I volunteered because I was the new guy and wanted the action/excitement that those hours had to offer. There were a lot of drug runners, stolen cars, and a bunch of drunk drivers to deal with on 17 back then.

This nearly 100-mile section of I-17 had the potential for officers to book offenders in three different counties-Yavapai, Coconino, and Maricopa. Since I worked out of Cordes Junction, I was familiar with Yavapai County, but not so much with the others. In fact, early into this shift rotation, I had never booked in either of the two other jails. Shortly after midnight on one of my first shifts, I was southbound on 17 at Black Canyon City when I observed a vehicle weaving and figured he was probable a DUI driver. I quickly lit him up, hoping he would stop in Yavapai County so I could book him in Prescott, but he kept going into Maricopa County before stopping. Of course, he was drunk. As I was arresting the driver he asked if he could have a smoke. I said no, he would have to wait until later. Now I had a dilemma. I had no idea where the jail was in Phoenix and I certainly didn't want to ask Dispatch, so I started driving to metro (at least I knew the Maricopa County Jail was somewhere in that general vicinity). After a few minutes of driving and worrying, I asked the driver, who I suspected had been booked a few times in his life, if he knew how to get to the jail in Phoenix. He said yes and he had been there multiple times in the past. I then said I would make a deal with him and told him he could have that cigarette at the jail if he got us there. He thought that was a fair deal and gave excellent directions, even avoiding some on-going road construction delays.

Since his directions were so solid, I allowed him not one, but two smokes before I booked him. A big thank you to all the Phoenix PD officers that night that took a rookie patrolman in and helped me through the intake process.

The Monkey

Randy Strong #1295

Back in the day, when Highway Patrol motor squads were needed in Parker, AZ to help control the crazies during warm weather holidays, there were many experiences that came from those details that were just as crazy. One incident that stands out most in my mind, and certainly needs to be shared, was told to me by Johnny Sanchez, #1463,

Johnny and his partner, Rick Williams, #897, (we usually rode in pairs on this detail) went to the River Texaco, a gas station/store adjacent to the river, to take a break and get something to drink. River Texaco was a little unique in the fact that it had some caged desert animals out front for tourists to see.

One of the cages, however, housed a monkey, which certainly would get your attention. There were signs inside the cage warning people not to get too close and not to feed the monkey. Well, Rick, being the curious sort, watched this monkey look down at the bottom of the cage and then look back at him. The monkey did this several times. This led Rick, of course, to wonder what the monkey was looking at beneath him.

So what does Rick do? Forgetting all about the warning signs, Rick steps closer to the cage to get a good look at what he wanted to know. In a split second the monkey grabs Rick by the hair and starts banging his head against the cage. The grasp was so strong that Rick could not get away.

As Rick was just about to draw his weapon and shoot, he broke free. The monkey just sat there feeling pretty proud with two fistfuls of Rick's hair. Johnny was laughing so hard that he could hardly talk.

Rick emphatically told Johnny not to tell ANYONE about what just happened. Johnny said he wouldn't. Well, we all know what happened next. Within an hour there wasn't ANYONE who didn't know. And we all knew that the sign in the monkey cage meant what it said!

King Kong

Rick Williams #897

There. It's out! For years I tried to keep this story quiet. Not that it ever really was. Anyone who knows me has heard this story. I finally gave in and said, go ahead and put it in the book.

I remember the day as if it happened yesterday. Johnny and I had stopped at the Texaco station and got off our bikes to go in for a break. There were a lot of tourists around watching us. We looked pretty good as usual.

As Randy said, that monkey kept looking at me and then looking at the bottom of his cage. Curiosity got the best of me and I walked over and looked down to see what the monkey was looking at. In a split second that monkey had reached through the bars and grabbed two handfuls of my hair. I had hair then.

He commenced to banging my head against the cage and refused to let go of my hair, Over and over my head hit the cage. Finally I pulled free, but the monkey still had two fistfuls of my hair.

It was a small scrawny little monkey but the minute he grabbed me, he became King Kong. Needless to say, I never again got close to that apes cage.

ROK Martial Arts

Johnny Sanchez #1463

Well, it was a typical day at the Phoenix DPS gym with tons of testosterone and jokes being thrown around. Some of the guys like Chuck Wright #951, Dave Johnson #689 and I had just finished working out, when an older woman and an Asian looking guy walked into the gym accompanied by someone from the DPS training staff.

The Asian guy was a pretty stout looking individual with hands like a hammer who was an X-military combat defense arts instructor, looking for a job as a defense/martial arts instructor in law enforcement. The woman was his sponsor while he was going through his immigration into the United States.

Dave Johnson #689, being a decorated combat vet during the Vietnam war, whispered to me these guys were pretty bad ass during the Vietnam war. About that same time, it was decided that this X-ROK soldier was going to give a demonstration of his abilities and they were looking for a volunteer. As luck would have it, we volunteered Chuck Wright since he was a pretty strong guy with lots of flowing testosterone. At first Chuck really didn't like it, but he wasn't going to let this little guy back him down. So, the ROK soldier looked at Chuck and said in broken English "he vedy-vedy strong," touching his pumped-up biceps. Chuck smiled with a look that said, "this guy doesn't look that tough." Next, the ROK soldier told Chuck to grab him from behind, pinning his arms to his sides and picked him up off the floor, squeezing him as hard as he could. After Chuck felt he pretty much had control of this individual he gave the go ahead to start at which time Chuck found himself being thrown to the fortunately padded floor. The ROK soldier started telling Chuck in broken English, "theese broke, theese broke and theese broke," pointing to the different body parts of Chuck. Of course, Chuck wasn't convinced so he gave it the old college try again with the same results, attempting to take down the ROK soldier again, but it looked like it hurt more than the first time.

I'm Going Where?

Greg Eavenson #680

I moved to Holbrook from Tennessee in '64 with my parents and graduated high school in'65. College for a year then joined the Army and worked hard to earn my Green Beret. Instead of Vietnam I was selected to fight insurgents in Cambodia, Laos and Thailand.

In Holbrook I dated Lt. Don Naval's daughter and got to know him which peaked my interest in the

AHP. I was lucky enough to get accepted to Class 15 which was the second DPS Academy but we still wore the AHP shoulder patch and were the last class to buy our own sidearm.

Prior to OJT, Lt. Ernie Johnson read out our duty stations. He called my name and said "Blythe". Blythe?? I asked Arizona natives on either side of me if they knew where Blythe was. Neither knew. I summoned enough courage to ask Lt. Johnson "sir where's Blythe ?" "It's in California, shut up and sit down ". Snickers were heard around the room.

Patrolman Keith Neitch 412 was my reluctant coach but did his duty. We caught a fatality on day one and it only got more exciting after that.

Our class graduated on Friday before Memorial Day weekend, and I was assigned badge #544. I also was the only cadet that been assigned a patrol car by Sgt. Larry Thompson 2 weeks earlier. My orders from him were to get my classmate Larry French (Salome) and head for Parker immediately after graduation.

We arrived midafternoon and met with Sgt. Alex Tolmachoff who assigned us to a coach working a roadblock at the curve south of Blue Water Marina. SR 95 followed the river in those days. Larry and I worked until 2 am seizing beer, etc. from juveniles.

I found Sgt. Tolmachoff asking what motel room we had. Unfortunately we didn't have a room. We drove 50 miles + down to Blythe to the converted garage apartment I had rented. All furniture was in boxes or crates so we threw a mattress on the floor and spent each night there.

We worked through the following weekend and on the trip to Blythe at 0300 Monday morning I called Patrolman Glenn Green asking if he knew when I was scheduled to work my break-in week with Patrolman Neitch. He replied that I was supposed to be 10-8 at 0500 today. We worked a relief shift with days off on Thursday & Friday.

Wednesday of that week we were to work 1400-2300 driving my car. I had to pick up Patrolman Neitch no later than 1345 as we had to be 10-8 in our area 15 minutes before shift. As luck would have it my wife and I were busy arranging furniture, etc. and I noticed the time was 1335 and I wasn't dressed. I checked 10-8 in Arizona and HP412 was also 10-8 at 1355. Before I could hang up the mic I heard "814 to 412". Oh Shit, that's Lt. Hoffman. He called again in a minute, so I had to answer telling him that I hadn't picked up 412 and was still in California. After a long pause he advised to get 412 and meet him at a cafe in Blythe. I figured I was fired and when I picked up 412 he was furious. Later 814 rode with us for an hour and still hadn't asked why I was late. I was sweating. After a traffic stop 814 asked me. I explained the graduation, Parker detail, no motel and having worked 17 days straight. He understood and never mentioned it again. WHEW!!

Another Scar

Bill Rogers #3578

I was stationed in the Globe Highway Patrol district and was a young officer assigned as a Field Training Officer to an even younger trooper. The officer I taught was very eager and able to complete the job. I was very proud of him and his efforts years later when he, on his own merit, became a patrol sergeant. I just hope I had some positive influence on that endeavor.

This particular night we were riding together as I drove. The DUI bewitching hour was approaching and we were ready to snatch up another one. We sat in the darkness watching the parking lot of a local watering hole. I never had a problem watching the parking lot for drunks. I'd follow them out of bars and observe their driving. I never created a false reason for a stop. It was dishonest and I never had to do it anyway. Of course I would also troll the roadways for DUI's watching for driving habits. But this night I felt like parking and observing.

As I watched from afar, I saw a young couple exit the bar arm in arm as they strolled towards their cars. I figured that they were going to follow each other in separate cars to a more private atmosphere, and that's exactly what happened. I watched as they got into their vehicles and she followed him out of the parking lot and onto a public highway. I pulled the patrol car onto the highway trying to be as secretive as possible.

It was not hard to develop probable cause to stop them as they both weaved along the roadway. My young passenger and I tried to decide which was the worst or best DUI to stop. We watched as both vehicles drove down the highway. They weaved in unison and were less than one car length apart.

When I saw the vehicles turn off the highway onto a county road, I saw a rare opportunity to stop both vehicles at once. I quickly processed a plan with my young officer to do this then put it into motion. The county dirt road was actually about a car and a half lengths wide. This meant that if we could get between the two drunk drivers the roadway would actually be blocked avoiding their chance to drive away from the traffic stop. I quickly out my plan into action, flicking on my emergency lights and passing the second vehicle hoping the first one stopped. It did.

I contacted the lead vehicle while my passenger contacted the rear vehicle. Although this was a tactical disadvantage for us, we maintained enough awareness of each other that I felt confident taking the risk.

The young officer dealt with the female driver. Meanwhile I dealt with the twenty something male driver. Together we removed them from their vehicles, conducted FST's and arrested both of them for DUI. The offenders were cuffed, with the female in the rear patrol car seat with the other officer and the male seat belted upfront with me. Once the requested tow truck arrived, both of their cars were removed from the scene. We were ready to head to the jail.

Up to this point both arrestees were somewhat cooperative. The female remained quiet. The male driver started out correctly but soon slid downhill as the alcohol and macho attitude took over.

He started by being verbally belligerent, increasing to a physical problem quickly. He was handcuffed behind his back and attempted several times to wiggle his hands toward the door handle, thinking it could be opened. At first, I responded by simply shoving his left arm towards the door forcing him to lean against it and thwarting his ability to squirm around. I did this as I was driving and it seemed at first like it was working. He started to increase his verbal abuse against me which I presumed was the alcohol increasing his bravo attitude.

He continued to squirm around and eventually I was able to grab the chain links of the handcuffs and force him to sit somewhat sideways in the seat. He had managed to wiggle around enough that I lost the grip I had on the chain links and my hand slipped so that I was only holding onto part of the chain and his hand. The drunk then twisted his torso so the rachet of his left handcuff tore into the flesh of my index finger. I felt the immediate ripping of my skin followed by pain. I became very upset!

While all of this was going on, I was still driving the patrol car, so I released my grip on the arrestee and grabbed my PR-24 baton with my left hand. This I carried on my left hip secured in the baton ring, and I transferred the baton to my right hand. I slid the long portion under the rear of the arrestee's armpit. I turned the handle to the left across his triceps and pushed downwards. This forced his face to his knee area and stopped his moving around.

Shortly thereafter we arrived at the jail. The female was processed by my younger officer without any trouble. The fight had been removed from my male arrestee and he even learned to say yes sir and no sir at the proper times. I processed him out of habit, having done this seemingly hundreds of times before.

Today, I look at my scarred finger and perceive it as a cost of doing business. It wasn't serious, definitely not life threatening. However, I still give thanks to God for all the blessings he has given me, those I recognize and those I didn't. All the times he protected me. hoping that I am worthy of his effort and his love.

What A Relief

Colin Peabody #481

Two patrolmen here in Phoenix got a call about a woman stuck in a Volkswagen who was unable to get out of it. They responded and found a woman well over 300 pounds stuck in the back seat of a Volkswagen and she was unable to get out. The officers tried and tried for quite a long time and finally managed to take one of the front seats out. During this entire time, the woman is telling them over and over again she is having a heart attack and can't breathe, having chest pains and breathing difficulty. When they finally get her to a point where they can get her out of the tiny VW and get her stood up, she expels a huge amount of gas. After a couple of moments, she said, " I guess I wasn't having a heart attack after all, I was having a fart attack".

I am sure Courteous Vigilance prevailed, preventing the two officers from offering their true thoughts about the matter!

Gib Duthie

Gil Duthie #1031

Gilbert "Gib" Duthie #143 is my father. Dad was killed in the line of duty on 5 September 1970 when I was 16 years old.

The Labor Day weekend of 1970 saw one of the worst floods in Arizona history. Dad received a call advising that Sunflower up on SR87 south of Payson had washed away. SR87 was closed and he was going to check if Sunflower was still there.

Unbeknownst to Dad, the bridge at Sycamore Creek just south of Sunflower has been washed away.

It was stormy that night and he didn't see that the bridge was gone. He went into the creek which was reported to be running 50 feet above the creek bed. His car washed about a quarter of a mile down the creek.

Sunday morning I had a feeling that something was wrong. My mother said that my father wasn't home, and I should go to church. I went to church by myself and on the way home, I knew he wasn't home. When I got home, I saw a lot of DPS at the house and I had a confirmed feeling.

Everything about that time is a blur. I remember bits and pieces. Everyone I have ever talked to says how great a guy my dad was.

I joined the patrol when I was 18 as a cadet trainee. When I turned 21, I went through the academy and was stationed in Globe. I also worked in Tucson with Liquor Enforcement and in Phoenix with Narcotic Enforcement and the DEA Task Force. I then moved to Prescott where I worked with the Prescott Area Narcotics Task Force until I retired after 28 years with DPS.

Code 20

Ralph Shartzer #220

I was working Phoenix Communications on the night that Gib disappeared. I was working the eastern section of the state from the small radio console off of the supervisor's office in the DPS communications. The state was receiving severe rain storms in the northern and eastern portions of the state and all patrol units were extremely busy checking on highway and motorists' conditions.

It was a chaotic evening with all the phones ringing off the hook in the communications center. My console phone was constantly ringing and officers were calling with changing conditions and asking for equipment and assistance from the highway department and other services.

As was procedure, a welfare check 'Code 20' was called to all units working. This was done every hour and, I don't remember the time exactly, but I couldn't get a response from DPS 143 Gib Duthie. All other units were responding but not Gib. One of the units stated that Gib had communicated to him that he was going to check the highway toward Payson and another unit was checking Payson South. A Code 20 was called to Gib every few minutes with no response.

I know that all communication and Highway Patrol supervisors were notified, and an immediate search began for Gib. I believe Gib was later discovered in his vehicle downstream from where a bridge had washed out.

1970 Sycamore Creek Flash Flood

Darryl Mullins #480

I was assigned to Dist. 5, (I-17, I-10 freeway). It had been raining all day on Labor Day, 1970 when I was advised to contact Sgt. Juan Martin. He said a flash flood had come down Sycamore Creek and took the bridge out on 87. I was told to station myself on the south side of Sycamore Creek at the bridge location. There were roadblocks set up on 87, but in case someone got through the roadblocks they could be stopped before they got to the creek.

I was told earlier that day Patrolman Gib Duthie had been on his way home in Mesa to get a change of clothes and a bite to eat, he then was going to go back patrolling north on 87. He was south of the bridge when dispatch advised there was a flash flood moving down Sycamore Creek and the residents of Sun Flower could be in danger. Gib turned his patrol car around and headed north on 87 to warn the residents of Sun Flower. Dispatch tried to contact Gib several times after that but he didn't answer.

It was dark when I got to the Sycamore Creek location and the bridge was totally washed away. I took my spotlight and shined down the creek and couldn't see anything but debris. I then shined the spotlight on the other side of the creek and noticed two indentation marks on the concrete embankment that held up the bridge. They appeared to be from where a patrol car push bumper might have hit.

I spent the night on the south side of 87 at the bridge location and Steve Hinderliter spent the night on the north side.

Thoughtful Citizens

Steve Hinderliter #453

The day we lost Patrolman Gib Duthie I was working the freeway in Phoenix. I don't recall much of that night, except that it was a wet, stormy night. Radio advised me of the bridge collapse on SR87 south of Sunflower and assigned me to go north and block the approach to the bridge. They advised that they had lost radio contact with Duthie. I arrived and took a position to protect anyone from getting to Sycamore Creek where the bridge was now gone. I remember sitting there all night and was extremely grateful for citizens who brought me coffee. The hot coffee was very much appreciated. When morning came, I took a good look at where the bridge had been and it looked to me to be gouge marks where the push bumper of Gibs car struck the abutment of the bridge.

Sycamore Creek Search 1970

Jim Bob Davis #734

The Saturday before Labor Day 1970, Arizona experienced some severe heavy rainstorms. At Sycamore Creek on the Beeline Highway the bridge had been washed out. Patrolman Gib Duthie headed that way but he was unaware of the bridge being washed out. In the heavy rain and due to the height of the flood water in Sycamore Creek, he was unable to see that the bridge had been washed away. He launched from the road and hit one of the bridge abutments and was killed.

I was in the DPS Academy (16), and we were called in to work in a search and rescue mission in Sycamore Creek upstream from the bridge. We were looking for survivors and victims in the debris . It was hot and humid in that canyon and I got heat exhaustion. We didn't find any casualties and climbed back up to the bus. We came back down to the bus and started searching down steam from the bridge area . About 130-150 yards down from the bridge we found Gib's gun & gun belt . Gib had remained in his patrol car but the water had so much force that it tore his gun belt from his body.

His weapon was still in the holster.

Forever In My Heart

Bill Rogers #3578

There I was, all of about 8 or 9, in the early '60's, squatted in the dirt of my front yard, when He came along. It was a bright Arizona day, where the sunlight could blind you if you dared to look up. I heard the car before I saw it, but quickly it was driven onto the concrete driveway of my house. The car was all white, except for the blue star on the driver's door. And then the driver's door opened...

I watched in awe, at first all I saw was this giant foot, from heel to toe, it seemed to be as tall as I was. Then his leg came out of the door, and the driver unfolded himself from the interior of his patrol car. I dared to look up into that bright Arizona sun, but it was an eclipse, as this monster of a shape blocked out the sun. The sun burst around His head, as he palmed his bus driver style hat, and plopped it onto his massive head. "Is your dad home", he spoke, as I wordlessly shook my head up and down. I jerked myself up, and ran to retrieve my dad from inside my house, as he watched me chuckling to himself.

My dad was at this time, a Reserve Arizona Highway Patrol Officer, and Officer Dick Wall #82, was his friend and mentor. Dad regularly rode with him, mostly on weekends. Dad was an Independent truck driver most of his working life, and as the story goes, they met when Dick made a traffic stop on dad when he was working. Over time, they shared life on the highways, and in greasy spoon truck stops, developing quite a friendship. There were times when Dick, and his wife Pat, would come to our house for dinner. Pat was a school teacher, as was my mom, which gave them a bond of friendship also. Dick was always kind to me, and I probably never spoke a word to this monster, as Dick was every bit of six-foot six, and just as wide, not fat, but overwhelming strong. Dick was a Korean War era veteran, a former Marine. And the way he wore his uniform, would have made any Marine proud, a poster boy look. The impression that he made upon me was unforgettable. His was an image that I wanted to emulate, and it was during this time that I actually started to decide what I wanted to be when I grew up. An added factor that contributed to this decision was my uncle. My uncle, Dick Savage, was Chief of Police in Wickenburg, someone that I idolized and listened to. He gave me solid advice over the years, I trusted and loved him. A solid respect for law enforcement, taught to me by my parents, was the kicker in my career decision.

Over the years, our paths would ebb and flow, as most friendships do. Dick would go on to retire from the Highway Patrol, going to work for Arizona's Interstate Commerce Commission. As luck would have it, his job was absorbed by DPS, and Dick became a legit "double-dipper" in the PSRS system. Assigned to the Terminal Truck

Auditors Section of the Commercial Vehicle Section of DPS, where we met again. I was assigned temporarily as his Sergeant shortly after being promoted, which created quite a chuckle from the both of us. This time remains to me a beautiful memory.

My temporary assignment led me to other details, and over the years, I lost direct contact with Dick for a while. Before long, he retired again, and I was then assigned to an area not far from Dick's residence. I knew that his health was failing, and I wanted to see him again, to tell him once again, how much his influence in my life meant to me. I won't ever forget stopping over at his house, seeing him and Pat. The big booming voice, the over whelming physique, the stories, and memories. My own father had passed away recently, and Dick gave me more stories about him to hold dear.

I always tried to make the effort to be a positive influence for young children, just as Dick had been to me. Who could have ever known what the future held? I have always hoped that I have helped some child, just as Dick did for me.

When I left Dick's House for the last time, he was walking slightly behind me. I looked over my shoulder to say good-bye, and I swear, as he stood over me, eclipsing the bright summer sun, he was once again in full uniform, as he palmed that old bus driver highway hat, and smiled down at me.

That was the last time I ever saw Dick. But he is, without a doubt, forever in my heart…

Skip Fink

Larry Scarber #3954

It's hard to believe it has been twenty-one years since a giant fell. My wife and I were discussing this sad anniversary of Skip Fink's death. I'm not certain Jeannie ever met Skip. But she certainly knew of him through me.

I first recall meeting Skip sometime between 1988 and 1990. I had just received a District Three Officer of the Year award. Within a month or so, I was contacted by Skip, who was working in Highway Patrol Bureau Staff (yes, it was a bureau before we started calling it a division). He explained over the phone that I had been selected to try out a laptop computer for writing my reports. It was a test program to see if there was a future for computers in the field.

About a week later, I met Skip at the Holbrook office. He presented me with a Tandy laptop. It was more like a word processor but was new and exciting. We spent about two hours together as I became familiar with its workings. Skip explained that the minimal orientation time was part of the project evaluation. He provided me with a manual and explained that I was to send copies of all my reports, printed on a dot-matrix printer, to him weekly for evaluation. He also instructed me to use it for personal letters and anything else I wanted to write, as he wanted me to become familiar with it over the three-month test period.

I was quite the novelty at the Navajo P.D. offices when I would bring my laptop in for writing my reports. I quickly learned how much memory a report took. The laptop had twenty megabytes of memory and I recall wondering how anyone could ever use that much memory in a lifetime.

At the midpoint of the evaluation, I was summoned to Phoenix to meet with Skip and review my progress. A question had been nagging in my mind: Why was I selected to pilot this project? A number of thoughts ran through my mind. Was it a reward for being the Officer of the Year? Or had he dug deeper and discovered that I received an award in the Academy for report writing?

We met in his cubicle on the 2nd floor of the headquarters building. This would have been around the time that Skip was serving as Chairman of the National Troopers Coalition. He was on the phone conducting business when I arrived, and he gestured for me to enter and make myself comfortable…on the floor. Skip's was the only chair in the cubicle.

After several minutes, the phone call ended and we began discussing the progress on the laptop project. He gave me the date that I was to return the laptop to him. At last, I screwed up my courage to ask why I had been selected for this prestigious (in my mind) pilot project. I assumed his response would be one or more of the many qualifications I had imagined. Instead, he said simply, "We wanted to get it into the hands of the dumbest Highway Patrolman in the most remote area. You were any easy choice."

Skip must have noticed the crestfallen look on my face. As I prepared to leave the cubicle for a long and deflated drive back to Kayenta, he gave me the first of many hugs I would receive from him over the years. It took my breath away…literally. And it popped some of the vertebrae in my spine. I often thought his business cards should have a warning printed on the back: "HAVE YOU BEEN HUGGED BY SKIP FINK? YOU MAY BE ENTITLED TO COMPENSATION. CALL THE LAW OFFICES OF DEWEY, CHEETHAM AND HOWE AT…" I don't recall ever seeing Skip again but what I got a hug. I felt accepted.

I worked outlying areas and Skip worked either at Headquarters or in Metro, so we didn't run into each other often. But the visits were memorable. I transferred to Gila Bend. While there, Russ Dunham allowed me to serve as a class advisor at ALETA in Tucson. Near the end of the class, Skip came down to explain the benefits of becoming a member of the Associated Highway Patrolmen of Arizona (AHPA). He was his normal irreverent self and I wondered how many complaints he generated. To say he was not politically correct was an understatement. Later, after I had promoted to sergeant, I saw one of his sergeants and asked about his complaints. He smiled and said, "Surprisingly, very few." I guess people just understood that Skip was being Skip.

While I was a sergeant in Coolidge, I was dispatched to a prison riot at the private prison in Eloy. The chickens had overrun the henhouse and were in control of the yard, having set a number of fires there. I initiated incident command and started calling in resources. At one point, I felt a hand on my shoulder and looked up to see Rod Covey, then Lieutenant Colonel of the Highway Patrol, standing behind me. He was not in uniform and explained that he had been visiting his daughter when the call came out. He told me I was doing a great job and he was not taking over command from me.

Eventually, the resources started to flow in. I was unceremoniously bumped from Incident Commander to scribe when Captain Terry Conner arrived. It made perfect sense, but it was still a little deflating to go from Grand Poohbah to a fetcher of refreshments and note taker. The Mobile Field Force assembled on the opposite side of the yard from our vantage point. Through my binoculars, I could see two warhorses, Skip Fink and Russ Fifer, lined up side-by-side preparing the march into the yard. A loudspeaker broadcast that the riot was over and that all inmates were to prone out on the dirt yard to be handcuffed. The officers entered the yard and inmates began dropping to the ground, peacefully allowing themselves to be taken into custody. All but one, that is. As fate would have it, the lone resisting inmate was squarely in the path of Skip and Russ. I was much too far, even with binoculars, to see their expressions, let alone hear their words. I could only imagine that they were ecstatic!

It almost looked like a cartoon when the inmate was taken forcefully to the ground. There was even a puff of dust rising off the yard where he hit. If anyone, inmate or DPS, wondered if Skip and Russ still had "it", they didn't need to wonder anymore. A few years later, when Skip's son, Mike, was hired by DPS, he was to be assigned to my district in Globe. I attended the Advanced Academy graduation in front of the Headquarters building. There was Skip, dressed in his Class A uniform and looking like the proudest papa in the audience. Prior to the ceremony, I cornered Skip and asked, "So, Mike has all your brains and brawn. But he has the tact you never had. Where did that come from?" Skip smiled broadly and said, "He got that from his mom!" Skip expressed that he was pleased that I would be Mike's district commander. What a great compliment coming from someone of his background! I got several hugs that day. I wondered if he knew by the bulging of my eyes when to release.

Fast forward to that fateful day, February 18, 2000. I was called at home by Phoenix OpComm explaining that Skip had been struck on the Superstition Freeway and was not expected to survive. I told the dispatcher not to broadcast over the air if Skip passed, but to send me "963" on my pager. I called Mike and told him that his dad had been in a bad crash and that I would pick him up at his residence in a few minutes. I was hopeful that Skip, who to me and many others had always been bigger than life, would somehow pull through.

Mike was stressed but hopeful when I picked him up. He told me his dad had survived what should have been a fatal crash years before. It was not to be this time. We had just passed the Claypool Highway Patrol office when my pager buzzed, and I looked down to see what I hoped I would never see. I broke the news to Mike, and we returned to the office for him to make a few calls before heading to the Valley.

We went to the house and I found a corner to sit in as friends, co-workers and family streamed in and out expressing their shock and paying their respects to Michael Ann and Mike. It's still hard to believe it has been twenty-one years. I miss the hugs. Rest in peace, my friend.

1958 Training vs 1961 Training

Heber John Davis #156

In 1958 I went to the Highway Patrol Office in Phoenix to get an application for the Highway Patrol. I was advised they were not hiring any new officers at this time. I then went to the Sheriff's Office and got an application to be a Maricopa County Deputy Sheriff. I fortunately was hired. My training consisted of 5 days in the classroom and one day on the pistol range. Then I was given a 28 Codebook (Traffic codes) and a Title 13 code book(Criminal code) and told to study them. My first shift was in south Phoenix. I met the sergeant at the old courthouse which was the Sheriff's headquarters. Our assigned shift was from 1400 hours to 2400 in south Phoenix.

At about 1600, we received a call of a fight and the suspect had fled the scene armed with a rifle and said he would kill the first officer that came after him. I found him under a bush, he was armed with a 12-gauge shotgun. I told him not to move or I would blow his head off, as I had my hand on my gun. The sergeant heard me and came over and cuffed the suspect. I never said another word until we booked him in the jail on the 5th floor of the old courthouse. My training was so inadequate that I didn't know if I should draw my gun or not. I didn't want to appear trigger happy.

I was so happy when I joined the Highway Patrol on July 1, 1961, that we received proper training in the academy. I was in Class #1 in the new academy building. During the nearly 16 weeks of training my class was saving money to pay for our graduation party. We also decided to buy a plaque in the shape of the state, with the names of our 3 instructors, Lt. Harley Thompson, Lt. Bud Kratzberg and Lt. Dick Raymond and all our classmates which we hung in the hall of the Academy building.

40 Years of Memories

Colin Peabody #481

I wrote the following in 2008 to commemorate the 40th anniversary of my academy class.

Monday, January 8, 1968

Well guys,

Here we are, standing in the east parking lot of the Arizona Highway Patrol headquarters, all of us in suits and ties. We are being ordered to line up by Sergeants Jerry Wenzel (RIP) and Dick Sandheger(RIP).

None of us really know what to expect from these two men, but the next 16 weeks will give us a fair idea. Yelling, hollering, slamming books on desks now unoccupied by the previous unfortunate cadet, just to name a few things.

On the morning of January 8th, we have marched into the Compound and now stand in line to have our ID photos made and our original AHP badge numbers issued. Each of us wore uniform shirts with the name tag "J.J. Gilbert; L. R. Wharton or H. James" (whoever the hell they were) and if the collar was too big, Sgt. John Gantt Sr(RIP). would stuff a partial roll of toilet paper back behind your neck to draw the collar up, then Rocky Harris (RIP)would take the photo. We would take off the shirt and hand it to the next guy in line who wasn't wearing one yet. Then over to supply to be issued our academy gear and back to our classrooms to find our desks and the load of books sitting on them.

We were then instructed as to how to stand up and ask or answer questions to or from our instructors. The guy with the deepest voice made an impression on me.

"Sir!, Mitchell, 383...................."(Now Mitchell, 477)

We will be inspected by Sgts. Sandheger and Wenzel in the parking lot each morning, march around in formation, then march down Encanto, raise the flag in front of the old headquarters, then march into the compound and be inspected--again, by the brass, Captain Pat McCollum Sr(RIP). and Lt. Bert Zambonini (RIP). Our starched khakis needed to have sharp military creases, our single AHP shoulder patch should have been creased down the middle of it, our leather gear(real leather, not that Corfam shiny stuff), boots, belt, Sam Browne and handcuff case highly polished and the brass snaps on our belt keepers needed to shine as highly as our belt buckles and hat badge. Our paper nametag had to be just so over our pocket. No fingerprints on the bill of our bus driver caps, either. After class and PT, we lowered the colors and were dismissed.

In the classrooms, whether we were in the main classroom or in the library, we were treated to numerous instructors teaching us all the things we were supposed to know once we were on the road. Oh yeah, the phrase, "If you can't cut it here, how ya gonna cut it on the road?" became part of our nightmares every night.

From Harley Thompson(RIP), Tom Mildebrandt(RIP), Pat McCollum Sr(RIP)., Dick Raymond(RIP), Bob Roller, Jim Tatum, Jerry Wenzel, Dick Sandheger, Harold Johnson (RIP), Superintendent Hegarty(RIP) and a host of others I have no doubt forgotten who they were or what they taught, we learned accident investigation, traffic law, some criminal law, Miranda (no one was really clear on that new one yet!), Arizona history, every state highway in the Arizona system, English, grammar and spelling, and how to write an arrest report beginning with "While on Routine Patrol...."

We had self-defense classes down in the basement where Vern Andrews rang my bell and made me see stars. We went to the range and Sgt. Harold Johnson (remember the nickname we gave him?) kicked several of us in the butt when we didn't shoot as well as he demanded. Guess he figured that if we couldn't shoot any better than what he saw, he was safe from us shooting him. Cal Vance (RIP) and Hank Shearer did their best to help us out. Cal even made arrangements with me to meet him at the city dump in Sierra Vista on the weekends after we both got back to town and taught me how to shoot or I would have been history.

We went out east of Queen Creek to an old abandoned WWII airfield to learn how to drive, taught by Red Hull(RIP), Hank Shearer, Harold Clark(RIP), Cal Vance and some of our class counselors. We learned how to change tires on worn out 1964 Fords as well. We took a tour of the ASP at Florence(It was called the Arizona State Penitentiary back then, for you newer officers).

We had unexpected evening visits by the staff to those of us fortunate enough to be quartered at the Coronet Hotel located at Central and Roosevelt. Bill Leach (RIP) was my roommate and Bob Bloss and Charlie Serino (Sr.) (RIP) were next door. Ron Delong (Sr.)(RIP), Jim Powell and Ben Smith were down the hall.

We took our weekly tests on Saturday morning and were released to go home but had to be back in town by Sunday evening. For those of us living 200 miles away, it was a quick turnaround.

As a car nut, I noticed some of the cars you were driving. Jim Bullard and Gene Babcock both had 67 Chevelle SS 396s, Dick Brost had a new Dodge Charger, P.T. McCann bought a new Plymouth RoadRunner, Dick Monell(RIP) had a 64 Impala

SS with a 409 engine, Tom Gara(RIP) drove a 59 Corvette, I drove a 64 Corvette StingRay, Roy Van Orden drove a new Porsche 912, Tom Ticer drove an old Studebaker pickup (which he probably still has). Charlie Serino drove a VW bug(I remember going down the wrong side of Grand Ave. in that thing one night), Ron Delong drove a plain jane 65 Chevelle, Bill Leach drove a new 67 Chevy pickup (we shared driving duties from Sierra Vista every other week) Ron Wood drove a new 67 Mustang, Ben Smith drove a Datsun rice burner and Chris Regan had a 65 Mustang. We all wish we still had those cars!

Some weekends our expense checks didn't make it in time, and we were forced to stay at the Coronet. I remember Bill Leach, Bill Barcus and I squeezing into my Corvette and driving to the McDonalds at Indian School and Central eating our one big meal for the entire weekend, 15 cent hamburgers and 10 cent fries because that's all we could afford. Driving a damn Corvette and couldn't afford to put enough $00.31 per gallon gas in it to drive to Sierra Vista! Just barely had enough gas to get to McDonalds and back. HAHA!

During the week, we would eat breakfast at Chris' Diner (Called Mel's now)on Grand avenue where two eggs, hash browns, bacon, toast were 89 cents and coffee was free since we were in uniform. At night we walked a mile and a half to Bob's Big Boy at Thomas and Central and ate cheap. Other nights, it was the Hansa House at 7th avenue and

Indian School for all you could eat smorgasbord for a couple of bucks. Lunch at the Peppertree at 7th Ave and Thomas.

When we went out on OJT, (FTO for you newer officers) we were well equipped. Thin duty jacket, khaki uniform with our gun belt but no gun, handcuff case and a paper nametag. I went to Winslow as did Ron Delong and Ron Wood. My coach, Bob Varner, may he rest in peace, made sure I had a snubby .38 to carry in the glove box...like I could have gotten to it quickly if I needed it! But he was thinking of our safety. One violator commented on my not having a sidearm to which the quick-thinking Bob Varner replied, " He's so damn tough, he doesn't need one." Yeah, right!

On Rt. 66, we investigated accidents every day. My first fatal came 3 hours into my first shift on OJT. I wrote and rewrote that report at least 5 times to satisfy Bob and Sgt. Bob Harvey(RIP).

Once back from OJT, we strutted our stuff. We were confident, we were proud, we were Arizona Highway Patrolmen. We got our patrol cars issued. They ranged from 1965 Plymouths and Fords, to 1966 Dodge Polaras or Fords, 1967 Plymouths, Chevys and Fords, all with the biggest engines available for police packages. We cleaned and polished our new rides, we sat in them and got familiar with where the switches were located and what they did. We went to a truck stop and got those neat switch extenders in various colors. We took the carbon out of a warning ticket and fitted the inside of the lens on the lights over those switches with carbon paper to dull the brightness of the lights. LEDs hadn't been invented yet! We put all our emergency gear in the metal trunk boxes and checked out our First Aid kits. My 66 Dodge had a full padded roll cage, rotary beacons on the Visibar, lousy brakes, gasoline transfer kit and a Frantz toilet paper oil filter. Messy damn thing when you changed oil! The car came equipped with a case of toilet paper and a shotgun scabbard in the trunk. The shotgun came with a yellow seal around the action that was grounds for termination if it was removed in between practice sessions at the range. You had to be careful when cleaning the shotgun and replacing it back in the scabbard so the paper seal wouldn't tear.

As you might have gathered from the previous paragraphs, The Arizona Highway Patrol began Academy Class #10 on January 8, 1968, and was the largest class the Highway Patrol or the DPS has ever put on. We numbered 85 on January 8th, with 75 new cadets and 10 AHP Dispatchers who would all become sworn officers on graduation Day, April 26, 1968. During the academy, we would lose 16 cadet officers, graduating a total of 69. (Since then we believe we have lost 26 of our class in death, with one line of duty death, that of Officer Bob Martin, AHP #110, DPS #474, on August 15, 1995). There are still about 43 of us remaining in various locations around Arizona and the United States).

Fast forward to the end of 2007, when the idea of a 40-year reunion of our graduating class was discussed. Several local guys we stayed in touch with were polled and the response was a positive one. We brought the idea up of combining the 40 year Reunion with the DPS Retirees Coalition Annual Meeting at a November 2007 Coalition meeting and received an enthusiastic response from them. Once the Coalition Annual Meeting date was set for May 3, 2008 in Payson, it was time to get down to business.

With the help of several Internet search engines and the Coalition membership roster we were able to contact 44 of the remaining members of Class 10. All gave positive responses that they would like to attend, however several were unable to attend due to prior commitments or health reasons.

On Friday, May 2, 2008, the group began arriving in Payson. Each was presented with a clip-on holder having their original ID photo in 3x4 inch size. Several fellows denied the photo was of them, as they were never that young, skinny or non-follicly challenged. Yeah, right! They also received an 8x10 glossy of that same photo, so they could actually see it was their picture, and one of our class photo with the names of the graduates on the back. That made it easier for us to find ourselves in that picture! Questionnaires had been sent out to all and the ones that were received back were collated, copied and placed in notebooks for each attendee. Each received a DPS Retirees Coalition coin. Photos of our class graduation were placed on poster board along with photos of our class members who had gone before us. Louise Woods provided photos of Bill on January 8 and on April 26 as well as snow photos of their Kayenta residence in the winter of 1968.

Several guys came from great distances to be with us. Sgt. Bob Bloss 460 came from Knoxville, TN; Steve Westra 949(RIP), came from Clear Lake, MN; Don Dickey 467, came from a small town near the Washington/Canadian border; Sgt. Vern Andrews 264(RIP) (Yes, honest to God, Vern was with us!) came from Las Vegas, NV. The rest of us showed up from various places in Arizona; Former Director, Col. Rick Ayars 457, Gene Babcock 458, Dave Boyd 461, Jim Charles 464, Charlie Cleveland 465(RIP), Sgt. Ron Delong Sr. 466(RIP), Frank Glenn 468, Sgt. Bob Harshman 469, Max Hyatt 26, Paul Koren 340, Bill Leach 473(RIP), Sgt. Paul McCann 475, Sgt. Bill Mulleneaux 479(RIP), Sgt. Colin Peabody 481, Jim Powell 382, Chris Regan 482, Sgt. Allan Schmidt, 223, Sgt. Charlie Serino Sr. 484(RIP), Garry Shumann 169(RIP), Sgt. Tom Ticer 490, Roy Van Orden 151, Don Wheeler 493, and Sgt. Bill Woods 496 were present and all of us had a great time.

The entire weekend was spent reminiscing, laughing, lying to one another, making jokes about each other and discussing our abilities to have survived on the road, 40 years of after-academy life in general and Internal Affairs in particular! No one can hold a candle to the late great animated Ron Delong when it comes to telling stories on not only himself but everyone within range. He kept us all in tears laughing at his versions! The numerous Coalition members attending the annual meeting and dinner had a great time mixing in with our group, telling more stories, as many of them were instructors in our academy, our supervisors afterward and friends through all those years. All in all, the 28 attendees had a great time and we agreed to do it again, although probably not in 40 years, since we are all in our mid 60s and early 70s now. While we might like to break the century mark, it probably isn't going to happen, but 5 years from now, look out! It is time for other academy classes from 1969, 1970 and later to begin organizing a 40 or 50 year class reunion, since we don't want to be the only ones to have tried it. We're just the first!

The Dozen

Paul Palmer #342

Reading Colin's story about his academy class got me to thinking of mine. We were the last of the male dispatchers to go through the academy. There were 12 of us. Not quite like the Dirty Dozen of movie fame, but we tried.

We ranged from me at 5'6" to Jerry Diehl and Ben Shumway both over 6'. We were quite a group. Ben had only one leg and Teddy DeLaosa had only one arm. It got confusing down in the basement during firearms training at the range. Sgt Johnson (Gar) would holler, "Weak hand only" and it would confuse the heck out of Teddy.

People came out of offices to see us march out to put up the flags every morning. Ben limping, Teddys sleeve flapping in the breeze and our counselor who would look up to watch the planes overhead, at times coming close to marching us into the gate. All we needed was a fife and a drum and the picture would have been completed.

You may be thinking, how in the world could these guys become sworn officers. We weren't the first. Previously, one dispatcher went through the academy in a wheel chair and another had one blind eye. And we all know that through the years, some cadets got through the academy with questionable intelligence.

We were a different group to say the least. Ben had 15 years on the department when the academy began. The rest of us had at least 2 years and we all knew the instructors and counselors. How do you strike the fear of God into a cadet with 15 years on the department? Old Ben had a "Been there, done that" attitude. We were respectful, but we were seasoned.

Our instructors and counselors were colorful characters. I remember Salt Jerry Wenzel who could become a wild man behind the podium. But then there was our counselor, Hank Shearer. What a gentleman! He got things on an even keel after Wenzel finished a fire breathing lecture on one topic or another. Lt-Capt.-Major, I forget which, Harley Thompson. A great instructor with interesting stories. Harley holds the record of a person being promoted and busted more times than anyone before or since. Capt. Dick Raymond taught accident investigation. His standing challenge was that if anyone ever caught him without a lumber crayon in his pocket, he would buy the coffee. I doubt that he ever spent a dime on that challenge. He would have the class stand by their desks and sing "Show on your field sketch only what you see". That little ditty occasionally runs through my mind even after 53 years. Harold Johnson was our firearms instructor. I won't say anything about him, but we were sure a happy group when he was gone and Cal Vance instructed us.

Our class being so small couldn't raise enough money for a big graduation bash. If I remember correctly, it was held somewhere in Scottsdale. Our entertainment was Lt Peso Dollar and his wife who provided us with some great country western music. He was the district commander in Globe at the time. Peso was known as the Singing Patrolman. I have two of his country western

albums, mostly oldies but a few of his originals, Highway Man being my favorite.
Our department has had some colorful characters and I am proud to know them and call some of them friends.

Dust Storm

Richard Richardson #188

Are you ready for an old AHP story about a patrolman that almost defecated his pants? Best grab a cup of coffee, ha! I recall one time that I was patrolling old US 66 in Aubrey Valley during the middle of July 1963. The valley is cattle ranch country and the highway was a 15 mile stretch of straight paved 2 lane road, located about 7 miles west of Seligman, Arizona. I happened to be patrolling the day shift in the area and noticed the air was very hot and dry, not unusual for this area. The wind was picking up and dust started moving across the highway. I had an idea this was going to develop into an area where bad accidents could happen. I might as well stay here and see what happens. At times the visibility was poor. In fact it was hard to see beyond the hood of my patrol vehicle. This can make for very hazardous driving conditions. The traffic was fairly light considering there were a lot of tourists on the highway at this time of the year. US 66 is a main travelled corridor between Chicago, Illinois and Los Angeles, California. Interstate 40 was just under construction through portions of Northern Arizona. The Seligman region was still being surveyed just south of Aubrey Valley.

I will always remember this day while on patrol because of a series of events that started shortly before noon time. I was driving eastbound at about 45-50 MPH, when the visibility allowed. The speed limit was posted at 60 day and 55 at night. I continued observing the wind and dust increase from time to time. The visibility became more hazardous as the minutes rolled past. I happened to see a vehicle coming up behind my vehicle. The dust was blowing harder and visibility was not good. The car overtook my vehicle. I sped up and followed it for about a mile traveling between 60-65 MPH. It was too fast as the visibility conditions were getting worse. I decided to stop the car and visit with the driver. I did advise him that he was traveling too fast for conditions and recommended that he slow down for his safety and those passengers in the car with him. He agreed and said he'd slow down. He informed me that he drove a bit faster in order to get out of the bad weather conditions. All I could do was shake my head slightly. I did write him a warning about the speed and he departed perhaps a better educated about weather condition driving.

I continued traveling back and forth within a few miles, observing the winds picking up even more and visibility decreasing to zero at times. I had a feeling that something was about to happen and it did. I observed a two vehicle accident that perhaps happened only minutes previously. A car bumped into the rear of slower car. Both vehicles had pulled partially off the pavement and were talking with each other when I stopped. I asked both drivers to pull completely off the road as it was too dangerous to remain where they were parked. They did as requested and the roadway was clear for other traffic to continue passing by. The visibility was always changing during the investigation. I completed an accident report, citing the vehicle in the rear for following too close. Both drivers departed the scene, and I continued my regular patrol duty.

I could see things weren't getting better and about a half hour later I came up on three vehicles stopped on the road, one partially on the pavement. Vehicle number one was driving slowly when struck from behind by a second vehicle going too fast for conditions. Then a third vehicle collided with the second vehicle, also driving too fast for conditions. The second vehicle was pushed into the first vehicle. I asked that driver of the third vehicle if he'd move his vehicle off the road and he did. Now I had multiple traffic accidents involving three vehicles. Fortunately there were no reported injuries. Everyone was shaken up and all three vehicles were still drivable. I felt sorry for the people in the first vehicle, as the driver was trying his best to drive according to dust conditions. I completed the investigation and all the drivers that they might stop at a gas station in Seligman and have someone check their vehicles to make sure their cars were okay to continue on their trips. With such little damage to any of the vehicles, I decided not to issue citations and advised each driver to contact his own insurance agent and file a report, let the agents figure out who pays for the damage done. How can one judge the speed when visual conditions can be such as they were today? There wasn't any high rate of speed involved, making it a judgement call on my part. I didn't cite any drivers.

I cautiously re-entered the highway and continued patrolling the area, as more accidents could happen as long as conditions didn't appear to be changing for the better.

It wasn't long and I came up on another two-vehicle rear end collision. Both vehicles were well off the pavement. The first car was drivable and eventually departed after my investigation concluded. The second car was not drivable. The elderly couple was still badly shaken up. I suggested that I take them to Seligman and have a tow truck come out later, once the wind let up. They agreed.

What happened next was not really a surprise to me, but I had hoped that I'd get the elderly couple to Seligman before something else happens. As we headed to Seligman, the Flagstaff dispatcher radioed me and advised that the a report from an Arizona DOT (Arizona Department of

Transportation) employee reported another accident near a designated milepost marker in the valley. I was about two miles east of that location. I informed the elderly couple that I had to turn around and answer the call. Each time I happened to look into the rear-view mirror, I saw the lady had her head down and covered with her hands. I don't ever recall her changing the position for a long time. I felt so sorry for her. She had to be absolutely terrified. Her husband continued to console her as best he could.

I headed west and drove as fast as I could, yet being extra cautious. I happened to see a bit of a clearing and what appeared to be something blocking the highway. My immediate concern was the safety of my passengers. I knew the road very well and that a barbed wire fence was 60 feet from the edge of the pavement. I slowly drove off the pavement at about a 30 degree angle. I had to stop three times to check where the fence was located so I wouldn't run through it. I finally saw the fence and stopped. I told the couple to sit tight, they would be safe there. I called Flagstaff dispatch and advised my location. I quickly said that I couldn't see anything at this time. I heard the screeching of tires on the pavement. Another accident was happening as I spoke with the dispatcher. I asked that roadblocks be set up asap in Seligman and Peach Springs immediately to stop all traffic from entering Aubrey valley. I still couldn't see anything because of the blowing dust.

At that moment my driver side car door opened. It was Sergeant James 'Emit' Wilhelm #711, from Flagstaff. He quickly asked what was happening. I informed him that I had just arrived and can't see anything yet. He leaned partially over me and grabbed the mike from my hand and spoke with a female dispatcher. She mentioned something about #220 requesting roadblocks. During that moment we heard a loud metal to metal crashing sound. In a split second his unmarked patrol vehicle came sliding near my vehicle, just missing the left front fender by only a couple feet and disappeared in the blinding dust. He had parked his vehicle on the pavement, vehicle in park, emergency break applied, and with a red spot light aimed to the rear. His vehicle had slid quickly past and just missed the left front fender of my vehicle and went through the right-a-way fence, into a pasture. I thought, 'What could have done that?'

He pressed the mike button and I recall his saying loudly, "My vehicle just went by, I think it's a washout, 10-4 on 220's request!"

The couple seated in the back, were still not moving and the lady still had her head in her hands. I decided to get out and see what was happening. I left the sergeant still talking on the radio. I still couldn't see anything, but headed in a 90 degree angle from the patrol vehicle toward the pavement. I managed to feel the asphalt with my shoe. For a moment I was able to see the back end of a tractor-trailer rig jackknifed, completely blocking the two lane highway. I did manage to see the advertising sign on the trailer's rear door, 'Navajo Freight Lines 'and the picture of the blue eyed Indian logo. I noticed that I was stepping on spilled diesel fuel. My next thought was the rig is involved and blocking the road, there may be more vehicles heading this way and could run into the rig. I determined to take a chance and try walking easterly on the centerline. If I could see any vehicles, maybe I could warn them about the road blockage.

I had a hard time staying on the centerline and seemed like an eternity passed by and not being able to see anything or vehicles coming toward me. I walked for some distance and then for a few seconds three vehicles headed my direction. I hoped that the lead vehicle driver would be able to see me and thankfully he did and slowed down. As the three vehicles slowed and opened their windows I yelled very loudly at each driver as they came by me. What I said was something like, "Get this @%#* car off the road and now and stay there!" and I pointed to the edge of the road quickly to each driver. I really must have startled all three drivers. They did as I said and quickly. I knew that I didn't have time to stand there and chat with each one that the road ahead was closed. The TT rig still couldn't be seen, and possibility of more cars might still be coming. I know after I said it, I felt badly but too late now.

I continued walking easterly, carefully on the centerline when all of a sudden, not being able to see anything, a white car passed by at a fairly good speed. I was lucky that I wasn't hit. I turned and the car was now out of sight in the zero visibility condition. I heard what sounded like a car sliding and then a loud crashing sound. I ran as quickly as I could, even past the three cars still parked off the road. What I saw as I approached the tractor trailer rig, was a small white car jammed partially under the trailer at an angle. It apparently tried to stop and was sliding on slippery diesel fuel and into the trailer. I approached the car and observed two college age females seated on the passenger side. The driver must not have had the seat belt fastened and slid over when the car started going sideways. The driver side roof and windshield, rear view mirror and steering wheel were sheered away from the vehicle. Had the driver been fastened in, she would have been decapitated. This is only the second traffic accident that I had ever investigated where being fastened in would have been fatal to a driver. The girls were shaken up and with minor injuries. I recommended they get out of the car and head toward the fence that could be seen at that moment.

I returned to the centerline of the road and walked for some distance, passing by the three vehicles still parked. I must have walked for some distance. I knew that the sergeant was checking for injured people. All I want to do was try and stop any further westbound cars from entering the scene. There were none. I hoped that the road blocks were now set and there wouldn't be any more traffic coming. By the time I returned the accident site, I met with the sergeant. He advised that the ADOT man was watching for eastbound traffic and stopping them at a safe distance from the crash site. The sergeant reported to me that there weren't fatalities reported and no serious injuries. He had checked all the vehicles and also called for trucks and ambulances, as many as could be sent and also backup officers to assist at the location. He said to me that he'd rather have too many than not enough. He also had checked with anyone that was involved for injuries. The sergeant did a great job with immediate first aid.

My next task was to take a clip board and paper then draw a rough diagram of everything I saw and collect driver's licenses, registration's and other information as I spoke with each driver and passengers when possible of each damaged vehicle. I sketched the vehicle positions, license plate numbers and area of damage to each vehicle. The people were very cooperative during the entire investigation. I also tended to some first aid as well. Several motorists that weren't directly involved with the series of crashes helped drive people to Seligman after I obtained the needed information from each person. I advised that I would be in Seligman and meet everyone at the first restaurant on the west end of town as soon as possible and return all paper work to the people involved in the accidents.

Other AHP officers arrived and assisted in handling what was needed. I told the sergeant that I'd head to Seligman and do what was needed there, then go to Flagstaff and make my report. He approved the request and remained at the scene with other officers. I felt fortunate to have such great help from fellow officers. I wish that I could have thanked each one personally, but there wasn't time at the scene.

I arrived in Seligman and observed the entire west side of the community was loaded with all sorts of parked vehicles, cars, trucks, busses, etc. The roadblock certainly did work. The restaurant at the edge of the community was packed with people. I entered and ask that anyone involved in the accidents to report to me and I will return their paperwork after chatting with each one.

About half way through the interviews, three men came up to me. I asked their names and started searching through my paperwork. One man said something to me that I'll never forget. He said, "I wasn't involved in any accident out here nor were my two friends standing here. We were the ones that you swore at." I was a bit shocked and wasn't sure how to respond. Before I could speak, he reached out his hand and grabbed my hand, he said, "You may have saved our lives by what you did out there, thank you." I still wasn't sure what to say. Several people in the large room were clapping. I immediately apologized to the three men for my language used at the scene. I said that it was the only way I thought of for getting their cars off the road and not get hit by other cars. I knew it was wrong, but time was of the essence. No complaints from them and no visit on thick carpet in the Superintendent Hathaway's office in Phoenix, my job was still intact.

There were eleven cars and one tractor-trailer involved in the series of crashes. I was able to determine that the entire mess wasn't just one accident, but numerous separate accidents. Totaled there were actually 12 different accidents because of multiple separate crashes involving two or more vehicles. One vehicle was actually involved in three separate crashes. Therefore I had to determine from the damage and the scale diagram how many separate accidents happened that afternoon.

I continued getting the rest of accident people taken care of. It was getting close to sunset and I had all that I needed to make out a report for the Flagstaff office. I knew the sergeant and a few patrolmen would still be at scene, finalizing what needed to be done. Regular traffic was now moving through the cleared highway.

Normally a patrolman would provide basic accident to the dispatcher over the radio. This was more complicated. Sergeant Wilhelm advised me to go directly to Flagstaff and provide the necessary information directly to the dispatcher. The crash scene was about 12 miles from Seligman. Seligman is about 43 miles from Williams, and Williams is about 34 miles from Flagstaff. The total trip would be about 89 miles one way.

As I drove towards Williams, my eyes were sore and I'm sure reddish from the dirt. I decided to stop at the Williams hospital and have my eyes checked. The ER nurse washed both eyes and provided eye drops. Once that was done, I headed on to Flagstaff and to the patrol headquarters. I provided the report as required. The District Lieutenant Ed Shartzer #809 advised me not to return to Seligman that night and that arrangements were made for me to stay with Patrolman Oscar Baron #50 overnight. Oscar was at the station and asked me to follow him to his house. I spent the night there and left the next morning after breakfast.

I arrived in Seligman about 1000. My sergeant told me to take the next day off and relax, knowing that I had the eye issue. I thanked him but went to work anyway. I returned to the accident scene. I wanted to draw a better scale diagram of the scene. I patiently did my measurements as motorists continued passing by. By 1500 I completed my measurements of yesterday's multi-vehicle accident scene. After I was back at my house, I drew the scale diagram accurately then superimposing the rough diagram to the new diagram that showing the skid marks, critical scuff marks, gouges, scrapes, and any glass and metal fragments still on the road after the tow truck people brushed the pavement. I mailed the diagram to the Flagstaff office as part of my report.

I did hear later that Sergeant Wilhelm stopped at the Williams hospital and had his eyes flushed. In fact he had a particle in one eye that could have resulted in the loss of sight. The hospital staff did a good job fixing his eye and he was okay.

I later learned that the insurance agencies handling their client's accident reports were very satisfied about the job that I did as an accident reconstruction investigator. Sergeant Wilhelm later informed me that the patrols training academy was using my scale diagram as a teaching tool for new cadets on how to draw a scale diagram. That did certainly make me feel good, however I was just doing my job as I was trained to do.

Over the many years I still think about that day of the dust storm and what happened. I'm truly happy that there weren't any fatalities or real serious injuries. A few weeks later a multi-vehicle accident happened during a dust storm on I-10 between Tucson and Phoenix. Apparently an oil tanker rig caught fire and there were several fatalities during a dust storm. My heart still goes out to those patrol investigators and citizens that were involved. Dust storms are nothing to fool around with.

1967 Snow Storm Problems

Rick Ulrich #182

Here are some snow depths that were posted about the storm. I can't believe it was 55 years ago. I recall bits and pieces of the storm, but I don't have a solid recollection of it.

The snowiest storm in Arizona History, started 55 years ago
Starting on December 12, 1967, back-to-back Snowstorms hit Arizona.
It snowed for 8 days, dropping:
99 inches on Greer
91 inches on Hawley lake
86 inches on Flagstaff
84 inches on Mount Lemmon
77 inches on Payson
46 inches on Prescott
48 inches on Morenci
2.5 inches in Gila Bend

The first thing I recall about that storm is that the road between Miami and Superior had to be closed. Not because of the snow, but because of a car sized boulder that landed on the road just West of Pinto Creek in the cut. The highway department said the boulder would have to be blasted into smaller pieces before they could remove it. Now, when the road between Miami and Superior is closed that is a big deal because it carries a lot of commercial traffic. The way around that closure is to take 177 South from Superior to Winkleman. Then take 77 north from Winkleman back up to Globe. SR-77 joins back up with US-70 just a couple miles East of Globe. The detour can add up to 1 1/2 to 2 hours for a trip from Phoenix to Safford. Not really convenient for truckers!

My next recollection of the storm was when Globe got hit with the really big snow storm. For some reason it took out all of our radios and microwave connections leaving us with no communications with all the highway patrol cars in Districts 6 and 7. That would have been about 90 patrol cars. We had no control of the transmitters on Signal Peak, Mount Ord nor Mount Graham.

The problem was on Signal Peak and Vern Worden, the radio technician, could not get up to the mountain to do anything about it The snow on Signal Peak was estimated to be about 5 feet deep. Vern had, as I recall, a four-wheel drive Jeep Wagoneer. It could traverse about a foot of snow, but 5 feet was a bit much. The Phoenix radio shop had a snow cat that they said they would try to send up.

We set a swing car up next to the radio room window and we could talk to the local Globe/Miami units car to car as long as they weren't more than three miles out.

The radio tech, Vern said he had a small transmitter tower, roughly 35 feet tall that he could erect temporarily just outside the radio room window. That would give us the ability to reach a bit further out with the local cars. Vern set that up and got us going again that gave us radio connection to about 10 miles from the office. It was not great, but better than nothing. Luckily, Phoenix and Tucson could reach most of the District six cars using the state frequency. Phoenix and Tucson pretty much took care of the District six needs.

The highway patrol office in Safford was originally designed as a dispatch center and had radio capabilities. Since the KAV 270 transmitter was still working it could be operated from the Safford patrol office. The only problem there was no staff to operate it. Sergeant Bill Chewning would go into the Safford office and act as a dispatcher for a few hours, but he soon found out that wasn't a really productive way to utilize his time. That area of Graham and Greenlee Counties usually had no more than one to three officers on duty at any one time. One officer worked out of Duncan and another officer worked the Clifton and Morenci area. Some of the officers had sheriff's office radios in their cars as back up when they were in areas where the patrol radios didn't reach.

When the really big snow storm hit, all of the roads to and from Globe/Miami were closed except US-70 over to Safford. SR77 was periodically open to Winkleman and Tucson, whenever the snow plow wasn't disabled, but the maintenance foreman for that area, Harry Mineer, didn't have the greatest equipment and it always seemed like he had snow plow problems whenever the first snow came. Harry Mineer was the foreman for US-60 East, SR-77 South and US-70 East. US-60 always had big snow problems at Timber Mountain on 60 and over El Capitan going South to Tucson on SR-77. Even if the snow plow trucks were working, there was always something wrong with their cinder spreader motors. Most of the patrolman in Globe can recall times when they had cinder spreading duties from the back of a snow plow using a snow shovel to spread cinders. Not part of their job description, but they did what they had to do to keep the roads open.

After a couple of days without radios or microwave telephones to reach other patrol offices, my job as radio supervisor meant I was sitting around twiddling my thumbs. The Globe/Miami sergeant, Jim Snedigar, seeing me doing nothing told me to grab my coat and rubber boots if I had them and come with him. The road was clear between Globe and Miami and West to where the boulder was in the road about milepost 238. Floyd Stiles was the maintenance foreman for that area and for some reason his equipment was always top notch and he was the first one to get the snow plowed up to the Top of the World. At the Top of the World, at milepost 236 was the Gila and Pinal

County Line. The maintenance foreman for Superior had responsibility for clearing US-60 West of the County Line. You would be surprised that the road from Miami to the County Line was always plowed and clear. West of the County Line to Milepost 227 at the East end of Superior was always snow packed and the snow plow was always late getting out. Funny what a difference the highway condition would be in depending on who was the boss over the area. One would think that was a challenge that could easily be remedied. The highway department has districts and each district has an engineer who was responsible for everything in their respective districts. The highway patrol had no authority to close any road without permission from the district engineer. The road might be physically blocked, but couldn't officially be closed without the engineer's permission.

Jim Snedigar tells me that he thinks we need to head out on US-60 East because no snow plow has made it down to Globe from Timber Camp. Jim has snow tires and chains on his car and we head out. I am not so sure about this because the road has at least a foot of snow on it. Jim's car is handling the snow so far, but if it gets much deeper I have my doubts. Jim is concerned that someone may have been caught in this storm and they need rescuing. His plan is to go at least up to Timber Camp. It is slow going, but we are making it. We get just a little East of the Elton Jones ranch turnoff and we could see a snowplow coming towards us. The snowplow driver advised that he came from Timber Mountain and there are no abandoned car between Timber Mountain and our location.

Jim opted to turn around and return to Globe. Jim said we would go down to El Capitan on SR-77 and see what the conditions were there. We could see that a snowplow had opened the southbound lane. We headed to the El Capitan area. We could see that the road conditions weren't that bad and as long as a snowplow was working the area the road should be ok. Jim wanted to turn around, but that task was going to be a little tricky. There was a pull out coming up on the opposite side of the road. Jim sped up and pulled into the pull out and attempted to do a spin around to get turned around. The snow was much deeper in the pullout and the car got bogged down rather than spin around. We were hopelessly stuck. We began removing the car's hub caps to use to dig the car out of the snow. As we were digging, a snow plow approached from the South and the driver saw that we had a problem. Using a tow strap and a chain, the snow plow was able to pull Jim's car out and we were back on the road again headed back to Globe. I guess Jim had had enough excitement for the day, so we went back to the Claypool office.

The next day was the third day with continuous roadblocks. At the time, there were only 5 officers in the Globe area and these guys were putting in very long days with so many roadblocks set up to advise motorists of road closures. The district commander had requested that Phoenix supply our area with some additional officers to allow our officers to get some rest. One person arrived to assist. This was Sergeant Frank Hutchison from the Tucson area. It is unknown what experience Hutchison had driving in inclement conditions. He was in Globe about three hours before he was involved in a 961A, which is an accident without injuries involving a state patrol car. That took an officer to investigate the accident and Sergeant Snedigar to go to the scene for photos. Instead of helping, Sergeant Hutchison was adding to the problem. There were some other problems he had with swing cars that he had to use while his was out of service.

I don't recall exactly, but it was about the fourth day of the storm that Denzel Wilson, the radio technician, came over from Safford and he and Vern Worden managed to use a snow cat and get up the mountain. It didn't take very long to get all the radios and microwave systems back in order. At last the radio room could resume normal operation.

It seemed like the storm went on forever, but I am told it was only 8 days. When the storm was winding down the temperatures warmed up and then it started to rain. Well, after all that snow, we didn't really need it to rain. There were all kinds of threats about flooding. The local National Guard was put on alert in case the flooding got bad. The Gila County Sheriff's office called the DPS communications center in Claypool to give us a warning of a possible breach of a dam at the Blue Bird Mine west of Miami. The mine security people discovered that the dam was in danger of collapsing. They said that in the event that occurred we should be advised that it may be necessary for all DPS personnel to evacuate the offices and go to higher ground. Oh great, after being down for over three days, here we go again. I contacted Phoenix to warn them that we may need them to take over our radio operations. After a few minutes I got a call from Colonel Tom Milldebrandt. He asked me who was working in the communications center. I told him it was just myself and Ben Shumway. Milldebrandt told me to get Shumway out of there. He said he knew that Ben had an artificial leg and would not be able to run in case that became necessary. I told Ben what Milldebrandt had said. Ben said he wasn't going anywhere. The two of us had reasoned that there wasn't enough water behind that dam to flood the Claypool area with more than a foot of water. We felt that we could handle a foot of water and maybe more. The pond in danger was about three miles away from our office. The pond wasn't like it was a huge lake. The sheriff stationed a deputy at the dam to watch it and warn everyone if it did collapse. Ben and I weren't really worried. The dam didn't break. Things went back to normal after that.

My Last Day As A Highway Patrolman

Ron Cox #1101

This story is about my last day of being a Highway Patrolman. I was transferring from D9 in Bowie to CI in Phoenix the following day. I believe it was on July 6 or 7, 1976. My shift began that morning at 0800. When I checked 10-8, I was told to go to the overpass on the East end of Bowie and assist Joe Olsen (RIP) # 699, with a 5 times fatal. On arriving, I find out that this fatal happened at 0600 that morning and should have been assigned to me. Joe was on duty in the Willcox area and told dispatch not to call me out, that he would take the call.

Apparently a pickup/camper had parked in the emergency lane E/bound to sleep, and an 18 wheeler ran right over the top of it full speed, and the cab of the 18 wheeler drove right up the sloping support of the overpass and wedged/smashed itself directly under the overpass. I think Joe headed back to Willcox around noon or so, and I directed traffic until the wrecker driver needed my assistance. He had lifted the rear of the semi-trailer up enough to find more body parts under the trailer. The only way I could describe it was a couple of large hunks of meat rolled up inside clothing. With a long push-broom, we were able to pull the remains to us without climbing under the truck should the wrecker hook give way. By the time we finished there, I believe it was about 1400 hrs., the wreckers were gone, the ambulances were gone, and as I looked around, I could see a dust storm beginning West of Bowie a few miles. I started that way and within about 3-4 miles, I could barely see the uprights of my push bumper. Every light I had was on and I notified dispatch of the situation. I was barely moving because of what I considered zero visibility. My goal was to get to Luzina overpass where the freeway went over the railroad tracks. I asked for a Willcox unit and a Safford unit to respond because from past experience, there was going to be pileups in both the eastbound and westbound lanes. It seemed like it took forever to get to Luzina. Tucson had dispatched Pete Cass #1248 from Willcox, and Bob Sabin #321 from Safford. When I got to where the w/bound was stopped, I pulled my car into the median leaving my outside speaker on as loud as it would go so I could find my way back to it. I then started checking the w/bound vehicles for injured folks. Pete was doing the same on the e/bound side. All totaled, if my memory serves me right, there were 17 cars/pickups, 3 semi-tractor/trailer rigs, and 1 motorcycle involved in both lanes.

Pete and Bob were utilizing ambulances from Willcox, and I found out later they were also commandeering motor homes and campers to transport injured to Willcox. There was not a single fatality. And fortunately, traffic was going slow enough that there were no major injuries.

Pretty soon the dirt quit blowing, and a fairly good rain was pushing it out. Around 16:30 or so, Pete found me. It was raining good but we weren't caring much. I'm still grateful to him to this day. He told me to go find my car and go home. DPS maintenance was sending two civilians to our trailer at 0600 the next morning to hook up to the mobile home my wife and I were living in and take it to Phoenix and set it up in a lot we had rented in Deer Valley. Pete took that pileup along with Bob's help, and that was the end of it. He wouldn't have it any other way.

I gratefully went back to Bowie, gassed up my patrol car, went home, and took a shower. Early the next morning, the two gentlemen from maintenance showed up, hooked onto the mobile home, and off we went to Phoenix. I was the lead pilot car with lights flashing, and my dear wife and our dog was the rear pilot with emergency flashers.

I can only say that the quality of people I have worked with, and for, at the Arizona Department of Public Safety, go far and above their obligations to not only fellow officers and their families, but to their dedication to their duties, and their desire to be of whatever assistance the public needs. COURTEOUS VIGILANCE indeed!!!

PS…the uniform was dry clean only. After the dust storm, and then the rain, it was no longer tan.

Well, maybe a very darker shade of tan. I believe it went in the garbage!

A Tragic, Chaotic Accident

Gary Ciminski #4575

When I was stationed in Benson, I was working by myself one night. About 1am, the dispatcher told me she had a call about a vehicle on the side of the road, possibly Code 34. It was at MP 328 on I-10 eastbound which was in the Willcox area, but their unit had gone home for the night so she asked if I could check on it. I told her 10-4 and headed that way. When I got to MP 328 there were three 18 wheelers stopped in the emergency lane. I parked behind them and started walking up to talk to one of the drivers to see what was going on. It was very dark in that area, and in those days, there were very few cars on the road at that time of night. There was no one in the first truck I came to, so I kept walking forward checking for drivers. When I got to the 3rd truck, there was no one there and as I was wondering what was going on, I heard voices coming from the median. I looked over and saw a very dim flashlight and three figures.

I crossed the highway and as I got closer to the drivers, I heard a strange noise. When I got close enough, I saw the drivers were looking at something on the ground where the noise was coming from. I shined my flashlight where they were looking and saw an infant about a year old and crying. I asked the drivers, "Where did this baby come from?" They said it was from the accident. I said, "What accident?" They said there was an accident in the median and pointed in the direction of my patrol car. I started checking the baby and the only injury I could find was a quarter-sized hole in the top of its head. I told dispatch as I ran to my car that this was a collision and there was an infant injured and to start EMS. I grabbed my first aid kit and went back to the infant. None of the training I had received ever addressed what to do for a baby with a hole in its head, so I took some gauze and put it on the hole to stop the bleeding and told one of the drivers to hold it there. I know that sounds ridiculous, but I just didn't know what else to do. It was cool, so I wrapped a blanket around the baby and then went to see about the wreck.

I went back up the median and found a Ford crew cab pickup with a camper shell on its roof. As I got closer, I started to find people lying on the ground. There were injured people everywhere, so I went back to my patrol car and told dispatch what the situation was. I told her to send ambulances from Willcox and Benson, and to call my sergeant, Steve Harris, and the on-call patrolman from Willcox. Basically, I asked her to send the world. I went back and tried to administer first aid, but almost all the people had serious injuries that I couldn't treat. As I moved around the truck, I kept finding more and more people, many of them children of various ages. I came on one man who was walking and didn't appear to have any injuries, but he was staring vacantly, and I could tell he was in shock. He was the father of some of the kids, but he was unable to help at all.

As I kept checking on people, I started to feel like it was never going to end. I almost lost it when I came to a boy who looked about 12 years old sitting on the ground. He had a nasty gash on the top of his head and was bleeding badly all over his face. I took a gauze bandage and put it on his head and told him to hold it there. He said he couldn't, and I told him, "Just put your hand on it and hold it on your head." He again said he couldn't, and just as I started to get upset, his cousin sitting next to him told me both his arms were broken. I told his cousin to hold the bandage on the gash and I moved on. I was starting to feel like the father in shock.

About 15 minutes after I called it in (the longest 15 minutes of my life), the first ambulance got there. I met the paramedics as they were getting out of their truck and started telling them about all the injured. As I went on, they got panicked looks on their faces. I really needed help because I was at my wit's end, and I told them so. They calmed down and started treating the injured properly, not putting band aids on like I was basically doing.

Pretty soon more help arrived, and the scene started to get under control.

The Willcox patrolman (I think it was Marty Bowlby) was assigned as the investigator. When things slowed down enough, I went and figured out what had happened. The driver, who was the son of the father in a daze, had told me they had a blowout. I figured he had just fallen asleep and was making it up as many sleepers did, but this time he was right. The right rear tire was shredded and what was left of it was wrapped around the axle. I went back up the road and found the marks where it had failed. After the tire blew, the truck hit the guardrail on the right and then veered into the median and rolled over. There were 6 adults in the 2 seats of the crew cab, and 9 children in the bed of the truck with the camper shell, so when it rolled people went everywhere. Interestingly, the pickup was very close to where I had parked my patrol car. It was so dark, and I was so focused on the 18 wheelers, I never saw it. This extended family was travelling from California to Texas, I think. The only fatality at the scene was the wife of the father I encountered. She was still in the middle of the front seat when I initially went through the scene.

They landed 6 helicopters that night along with I don’t know how many more ground ambulances. Amazingly and sadly, the only other fatality from this wreck was the baby. It didn’t survive at the hospital, and to this day I don't know whether it was a boy or girl.

Funeral Service en Route

Steve Gendler #1064

In 1973 accident response in a rural area was nothing like it is today. There were no paramedics or medical ambulances in the Picacho area of District Six, and the Eloy funeral home's "ambulance" was used for transportation of the injured. We also didn't have portable radios so when you were away from the car you had to set your outside speaker on high to hear the dispatcher. So it was on a brisk fall night when I was dispatched to an accident with injuries in the desert darkness between Picacho and Red Rock on I-10.

As I rolled up with lights flashing I could see it was a mess. A pickup with passengers and their belongings in the bed had over corrected and was on its side blocking all traffic with people laying on the pavement and clothing, food, furniture and debris scattered all over the roadway. Grabbing my first aid box and requesting a tow truck and ambulance I turned my outside speaker up all the way and rushed to scene. There I found two dazed children with superficial injuries and their distraught mother with cuts and bruises wailing wildly and running around in circles from the truck to the children screaming “he’s dead, he’s dead”. The father was still in the truck and when I climbed in I found him with possible broken bones and profuse bleeding from cuts in his face and head which I handled - but he was definitely not deceased. My biggest problem as I climbed back out of the truck was to get the scene in general and the hysterical mother specifically, under control. I was finally able to settle her down somewhat with the assurance that her husband would be ok which was working until the outside speaker on my patrol car blared the following “1064 be advised that ***Valley Funeral*** is 10-19”.

CAR 54 Where Are You?

T.K. Waddell #803
Gamble Dick #1743

On a cool, dark, starry night, somewhere west of Seligman on US-66, while I was playing with my CB radio, I received a car-to-car call from Gamble Dick, HP-1743. Hey TK, can you 45 me at around MP-126? Sure, be there in a few. Upon arriving in the area, I didn't see Gamble, so I drove a short distance further, thinking he may have mistaken the location. Well, after a few more minutes of driving in both directions, I didn't see him or his vehicle. Again Gamble called, hey are you close by? Well, I said that I drove by the location in both directions and didn't see you. Have you moved or changed your mind on the 45? No, check out the Eastbound side at MP-126 just past the guard rail. As you will read further, it's a good thing we had car-to-car radio.

I stopped my vehicle, got out of the car and walked around. It was quite an eerie feeling, a very dark night with a slight cool breeze and the silence of the high desert. Then, just like a cheap stereo radio (back when I could hear out of both ears) I heard the crackle of Flag radio as they started their code 20 checks. That's weird, I'm hearing two sounds, one on the left and one right? With that, I took my trusty never dependable Eveready issued flashlight, banged it a couple times and looked over the roadside edge. There he was! I saw Gamble and the top mounts of his vehicle! He was about 15 feet down, over the side of the roadway. I yelled down, "How the Hell did you get down there"! Gamble shouted, Hey have radio call Murphy's towing for a Code 34. Don't tell them it's me! Just get him out here.

Ok, ole buddy will do, trying to keep my composure and my voice calm, as I radioed Flag on district. (We did not have cell phones back then.)

Well, Gamble explained: I saw a Code 34 changing a tire on the roadside. The guy was using a bumper jack at the rear of his car. I decided to pull up behind him and put my push bumper against the rear of the car so it could not roll back and fall off the jack. Well after changing his tire,

(all good officers did that stuff back then) the driver thanked me and drove away.
This is where the story gets good.
After that, I returned to my car and began to back up a short distance to get enough room to make a U-turn, (old 66 was very narrow). As luck would have it, as I backed up I began to slide over the soft roadside edge. I tried desperately to pull forward and maneuver onto the roadway, but kept sliding down the cinder embankment. So there, that's how I got there, and that's my story!
Well, just after Murphy's 926 pulled Gamble to safety, a timely code 20 on 1743 was heard and Gamble calmly responded, Code 4, MP-126.
Well, to the best of our feeble memories, everything worked out OK. No damage to the vehicle, no tow charge and no mention of this, until NOW! Just a bit of humiliation on Gambles part. But as we all know many things like this did happen, and are still locked away in our memories, or until another book is published.
By the way, Gamble, you still owe me that hot cup of coffee!

That's My Vehicle!

John Fink #683

One year DPS Air Rescue had a statewide unit meeting in Casa Grande. I flew to Casa Grande in the helicopter from Tucson rather than drive.

After a full day of meetings my Sergeant, Sam Fragala, bumped me from the helicopter and asked me to drive his DPS vehicle back to Tucson. Officer/Paramedic David Madrid also flew with Sam in the helicopter back to Tucson.

David relayed the following information to me - while flying back to Tucson they spotted a vehicle heading South on I-10 at an exceedingly high rate of speed. They notified dispatch to have a unit intercept the vehicle as they descended to keep track of the vehicle. As the crew got closer David told me that Sam hollered "that's my vehicle!". Needless to say they called off the vehicle intercept. I don't exactly remember the speed at which I was going but I do know that I came close to beating the helicopter back to the airport!

I'm pretty sure that was the last time Sam asked me to drive his vehicle!

I Bought A New Set of Tires

Dick Lewis #176

I came on the Arizona Highway Patrol from the Tucson Police Department. I graduated in class #2 and was assigned to my hometown of Globe. I was really born in Pima, Arizona but grew up in Globe and went into the U.S. Navy when I was 18. So, that is why I ended up in Globe.

Jim Snedigar #712 was a patrolman up in Holbrook when he was promoted to sergeant and transferred to be the sergeant in our area. My original badge number was #194.

I was assigned as an FTO or at least one of them in the area.

At this time I am writing about, there was a newly assigned officer riding with me. We were on night shift and it was after dark and we were sitting broadside on US70 east of town. Sergeant Snedigar drove up and got in the back seat of my car with me and this new officer. We were talking shop and the sergeant was asking this officer questions about how he would handle different situations.

He asked this officer, "What would you do if your mother drove by and was speeding?" The officer answered in a very official and gruff tone, "By golly I would stop her and write her a ticket."

The sergeant asked me the same question. My reply was, "Nothing." Sergeant Snedigar said, drawing out the word well, "Weell, let me tell you a story."

I was working up on the old 66-I40 out of Holbrook one day when I fell behind a line of traffic. Up ahead I saw a vehicle passing and making its way up to the head of the line. It was speeding when I got up there and when I got it stopped, I recognized my young and beautiful wife as the driver! She was test driving a vehicle she was going to buy, and I didn't recognize the vehicle.

The officer asked, “Did you write her a ticket?” The sergeant said, “Nooo! I went to town and bought a new set of tires for that car. If Lorna Mae was going to drive that fast, I wanted the car to be safe!”

Shiftless

Rick Williams #897

I believe it was 1978 when myself, Bob Halliday #1255 and Gary Fitzsimmons #574 were instructing a motor school. When it came time to take the students on their first ride, Gary got the loan of a Honda Goldwing motorcycle which Honda wanted to test to see if it was functional as a police bike. I got the Goldwing to ride.

Off we went on our ride with Bob and me following the group. All the way from Phoenix to Cave Creek, Bob kept asking me to let him ride the Goldwing. I kept saying later. In my mind, I had planned to swap bikes in Cave Creek, but I didn’t say anything to Bob. I kept stringing him along. Over and over he asked.

When we got to Cave Creek, it started to sprinkle rain. There was no traffic, so we stopped in the middle of the road at the intersection at the Texaco station. When I put the bike in neutral I heard a clink and looked down and saw that the shift lever had fallen off the bike and was laying on the pavement. I’m supposing a pin came loose in the lever. I got off the bike and motioned for Bob to take the Goldwing. At this time two cars pulled up behind us so we were in a hurry to move the bikes. I got on his bike and rode over to a dirt pull off. It started raining hard now so I rode over to the Texaco station. Bob was going to follow me to the station out of the rain. He tried to shift and looked down and saw the same thing I saw. The shift lever laying on the pavement. He had to push the Goldwing off the road into the station. There is nothing more embarrassing that being in full uniform pushing a police motorcycle.

To this day Bob still thinks I sabotaged the bike. It was all innocent on my part, except not telling Bob about the shift lever before I took over his motorcycle.

Too Many Utensils

Frank Glenn #468

This is just a funny story. In 1974 the department sent Mel Risch, Charlie Sanders, Ed Teague, Ken Chlarson and myself to the international police Olympics in San Francisco. We had a great time and won several medals. One night I think it was Mel who ask the concierge of the hotel were staying at where we could walk to get a good steak. He went on to give us some directions and told us to not go past 12th street, I don't even go there (he was a black man). Well, we take off and took a wrong turn somewhere and wound up on a street which looked like pimp city, guys in funny clothes and all manner of outlandish dress. We were all just standing looking around with our mouths open starring at the show. Two SF cop cars showed up in just a few minutes and they got out and said "what the hell are you guys doing here?' We told them and they said get in and took us to the restaurant and said "when you leave call a cab." Did I forget to mention that there was a room where we could get free drinks at our hotel? Well, I had had a few and was not drunk but let's say I was felling no pain. When we sat down there more knives, forks and other tools for eating than I had ever seen before, a bunch to the right and left and even at the top of our plates. The waiter walked up with a towel over his arm and my mouth got going and I said "what are you doing with that rag over your arm?" he was a bit taken aback but said "if I tell you there is going to be blood shed". I said yours or mine"? No reply from him. So, we ordered and when he came back to bring our salads, I said "I have another question for you?" Now he is somewhat wary of me not knowing what was going to come out of my mouth. But said what do you want to know? I said "these guys tell me that I am supposed to work my way in using these tools working from the outside in. Is that correct?" His reply was to say "Well sir I am a bit surprised that you would use a fork at all." There were only 3-4 other tables of people sitting there that had been listening to my conversation with the waiter and when he said that the whole house came down with everyone laughing including me. It was a great time and I boosted his tip up a bit for the comeback with me.

Smells Like A Skunk

Louie Chaboya #1139

Another story about George Rider (The Prankster). Rudy Acevedo was provided with a brand-new patrol car. One day Rudy was in the office and George also went to the office and asked Rudy if he could test drive the new patrol car. Rudy working on a report said yes and gave George the keys to the patrol car. George then took the keys, got in the patrol car and headed north on I-19. He went about a mile north then crossed the median and headed back to the office. As he was approaching the exit ramp off I-19 he ran over something on the shoulder of the road. What happened before George got to the office to ask Rudy for his patrol car is that George noticed a dead skunk and though "Hmmm, let's see what I can do to Rudy's new patrol car".

George got back to the office and gave the key's back to Rudy stating that the patrol car really drove great BUT, that it sure did not smell good. Both went out to the patrol car and Rudy noticed part of the skunk on the side of the car. Yep Rudy had a few choice words for George that I cannot print. Gorge did help Rudy wash down the patrol car, but Rudy obviously did not like George on this occasion.

Curley Moore

John Underwood, #419

When I first met Curley Moore… I have no recollection of the year, I was fairly new, but I was assigned to Prescott for Rodeo Days along with several other patrolmen. We were housed in some no-tell motel in the City, and it certainly wasn't a Marriott. As I recall there were four of us in the motel room, and I was on a cot the management threw in the door.

In late afternoon we met in the room for a briefing, and in walks Sgt Curley Moore who takes up residence on the end of my cot. A jovial guy so I immediately thought I am really going to like working for this guy. The briefing started and soon after the good Sgt reaches under my covers and pulls out several bobby pins…. What is this he bellowed at me!!! You've had a woman in this bed. And then he proceeded into a phony tirade about not having women in the room… I was floored!!! Where did those come from?? How in the world did they get in my bed??? Soon Curley left the ass chewing and continued with the briefing. Shortly thereafter he reached in my bed and out came more bobby pins, and more, and then the start of another ass chewing, (I was mortified), until he broke out into loud laughter along with everyone else in the room. I think the blood drained from my body, and then I too started to laugh after realizing "I had been had by the famous Curley Moore". What a great guy, and we were friends ever after, but any time we met up he would go out of his way to remind of the bobby pin incident!

The Horse Pasture

Don Barcello #515

I thoroughly enjoyed my time on the governor's detail. I saw places I would probably never had seen otherwise and met some interesting people.

Usually when you traveled with the governor, we had nice hotel accommodations. That is unless you had the assignment to take Governor and Mrs. Castro to their property in Prescott. Then, there was no luxurious hotel.

Our accommodations in Prescott was a state trailer parked in a horse pasture next to the residence. Mrs. Castro loved horses. The department had a spare trailer and parking it on the Castro property was free.

On those trips you knew you were not going to get a full night's sleep. Each night in the middle of the night, a horse would begin scratching itself on the corner of the trailer. This happened without fail. The trailer would begin rocking like a ship in a typhoon. Sleep was out of the question.

You counted the hours until the time came to take the Castros back to Phoenix and you could finally get a full night's sleep.

How I Almost Shot 2 Hitchhikers

Dennis McNulty #1959

I was assigned to District 3 Winslow squad in September 1981. Thad Hale #685 was my 1st Sergeant and, for my FTO period, I was assigned to be trained by Bob Varner #438 and whispering Bill Holden #684, who was stationed in Heber. I had great fun with both of them and learned a lot.

So here I was, cut loose as a solo patrol officer. On my 3rd day out on my own, I was working the 06/14 shift out of Winslow. That morning it was light traffic and I had stop a violator for speed westbound on I-140 near Hibbard Road overpass. I was writing him a warning when we both heard a semi-truck horn blowing from behind us. A Yellow Freight set of doubles slides to a stop next to my unit in the slow lane (thankfully very little traffic). The driver jumps over to the passenger seat in his cab, rolls down his window and yells out "Hey trooper, right back at the Jackrabbit Road overpass westbound, right at the top of the bridge, there are two women hitchhikers sitting on the guardrail and one of them pointed a .45 auto at me when I passed them by." This was a first for this rookie so I told the trucker to continue on, gave the violator his license back and took the 1st crossover to go back east. I radioed the info to Flag Opcom and, as I went over the eastbound Jackrabbit Road overpass, I saw the two women still sitting on the westbound guardrail. I took the next crossover, turned on my lights and pulled to a stop near where they were sitting. Upon exiting my car and using my best highway patrol voice, I ordered them to put their hands up. They just stared at me. I repeated the hands up command with louder volume with the same result, so I drew by service revolver, pointed it at them and really yelled for them to put their hands up. I distinctly remembered that I had my finger on the trigger with pressure. At that point in time one of the women made a sound, the kind of sound that once you hear it, you know what it meant. My brain kicked in and said "deaf mutes". I holstered and mimicked speaking to which they both shook their heads. One of them then produced a business card that most deaf folks carried that explained their handicap. OK, out came my pocket spiral note pad and I told them why this crazy cop had driven up on them. They told me and I retrieved out of one of their backpacks, a 3/4 size exact replica of a Colt .45 auto pistol that was a cigarette lighter one of them had bought at one of the state line tourist stores. You pulled the trigger to get of flame but instead of the flame coming out of the barrel, it came out of the ejection port so that when you went to light your cigarette, it did look like you might be pointing it at someone. I asked them to please not do that again, told Flag Opcom it was code-4 and then drove to the Winslow office where I sat down in the office to calm down and contemplate the possible newspaper headlines about a rookie highway patrolman who shot and killed two deaf mutes for not listening to him.

The Tortillas

Tim Hughes #793

In 1971 or 1972, I had to take my vehicle into Phoenix for service at the shop. I was stationed in Salome at the time. In those days, if we had a vehicle serviced at the shop, they would try to loan us an unmarked vehicle do whatever, while our vehicle was being serviced.

I went to El Molino on Washington Street and picked up probably about 6 dozen large tortillas for the families in Salome. El Molino had great tortillas and were a real treat in Salome.

On my way home, I came upon a 962 between Sun City and Wickenburg. After determining there were injuries, I called for an ambulance and went to my trunk to get my first aid kit. I had a gentleman bystander at the rear of my patrol vehicle when I opened the trunk and there sat a large pile of tortillas. The gentleman looked at me and said, "you Highway Patrolmen really are ready for anything aren't you".

After leaving the accident and returning to Salome, I distributed the tortillas to those who ordered them and all was well.

Gone In 60 Seconds

T K Waddell #803

In 1978, auto theft in Arizona was rampant. DPS and other agencies had assembled auto theft squads in an attempt to address the numerous vehicle thefts throughout the state. On one occasion I was sent to Tucson to assist the Tucson Police Department along with Neil Hanna and Paul "CUB" Nixon who were assigned to our auto theft squad in Tucson. Tucson had significant losses primarily due to the stolen vehicles being driven across the border to Mexico, primarily Ford F150 trucks.

One memorable evening, the Tucson PD used a recovered stolen F150 as a bait vehicle. The Tucson PD detectives convinced the insurance company, who now owned this vehicle, to use it as a bait car for their auto theft enforcement. The F150 was well equipped, having a very nice paint job as well as a mural of a Comanche Indian Chief painted on the driver and passenger doors.

DPS radio techs installed a low power radio activated ignition cut off switch having a 2 block radius. The transmitter was activated by keying its microphone through the DPS radio system. This cut off device was not visible to a thief, and would not hinder normal vehicle operation until activated. The bait vehicle was parked in the parking lot of a local movie theater at the Tucson mall. This location was selected because a thief would know that the owner would be away from their vehicle for a few hours while attending a movie. Also, this is a high stolen vehicle area and provided a car thief a vast selection of vehicles to choose from.

Upon parking the bait vehicle, the TPD detective walked a short distance to our staging area for our evening briefing. From our position, we could all watch the bait vehicle and respond on short notice, should we see some activity. Sgt Monk, TPD, was a chess game buff. He brought a portable chess game and began playing chess, with us watching. There were about 7 officers on the detail, and we had just started watching Sgt Monk, when one of our team members said, "HEY, WHERE IS THE BAIT CAR?" WHAT? We all looked over towards the area where the vehicle was parked, and sure enough, it was GONE! What the ......! It certainly was gone. None of us thought the vehicle would be stolen so quickly. Nobody in our team saw it drive away. Well, so we thought.

One of the TPD detectives had parked directly in front of the bait car. The TPD detective watched the thief steal the vehicle, but could not contact the team since he didn't have a portable radio. The bait car hadn't been parked more than 5 minutes before the thief drove it away.

Dave Smith, yes, the same Dave Smith now a retired DPS LT, was responsible for the safe keeping of the vehicle, and was about to have a heart attack! Neal Hanna immediately grabbed the microphone, attempting to deactivate the vehicle's ignition.

Sgt Monk was yelling to the PD dispatcher trying to describe the vehicle. "It's a brown Cherokee Comanche Chief" with Indian markings on the doors! Well, not exactly a good description of the Ford F150, but in the heat of the moment, it would have to do. Dave Smith and Neal Hanna attempted to correct the vehicle description through DPS radio and Tucson PD dispatch, which further confused the issue.

We did not know how far the thief could travel in the short time that we missed seeing the vehicle, but it had better be within the 2 block radius! Notify all marked units in the area!! Call the Port of Entry, we have to find this vehicle! Every team member jumped into their cars and began a sweep of the neighborhood. Back and forth, in and out, no sightings. The car to car radio traffic was buzzing, where is this thing? We looked like the Keystone Cops movies. Panic was among all of us! The Bent Screwdriver Award was about to be awarded to the entire team!

Finally, a unit radioed "WE FOUND IT" The driver's door was open, and the engine was dead! No damage, but no suspect to be found in the area. Luckily, the kill switch worked a little farther than the advertised 2 blocks. The truck was found approximately 4 blocks away in a residential neighborhood just south of the Tucson mall. Neighbors living across from where the vehicle had stopped, saw the thief attempting to do a restart and trying to fix the problem with no luck. They provided a good description of the thief thus providing for an arrest at a later date.

Dave breathed a sigh of relief, and wouldn't have to pay for a lost bait vehicle. Even after 40 years, this would be an evening to remember by all of us on that detail. For those of you who don't know Dave by his real name, does Buck Savage sound familiar?

The Gift Of Gab

Darryl Mullins #480

I had been assigned to the Fugitive Detail for about four years and was in the office with Sgt. Alan Wright one day when he received a phone call. Shortly after he started talking on the phone he motioned for me to come over to his desk. When I got to his desk he covered the mic and whispered, "Escapee, and gave me his name. He talked to the suspect some more than whispered for me to get a trace on the phone call with an address. I contacted the phone company, and after 20 minutes of going through different supervisors I was able to get the address. I showed Sgt. Wright the address, he was still on the phone with the suspect, he turned and pointed for me to go. I and another agent who was in the detail temporarily, left the office, which was on the 2nd floor of the old MVD building, across the street from DPS headquarters. We were each in our own unmarked cars. I was going down 19th Ave, weaving in and out of traffic with no emergency lights on. I would get hung up at intersections and when the light changed, I was off again. I got to where I thought I could go unobstructed at the Salt River Bed when I looked up and saw there was a roadblock. I pulled up to a Phoenix Motor Officer, showed him my I.D., told him what I was doing, his response was, "Can I go with you", I told him he could go but not code 3. So we took off with the motor officer and a marked P.D. car behind me. We went down Broadway to 9th Ave., went down a couple of blocks down and to the address. I got out, went up to the front door, with the PD Officers behind me, I knocked on the door and when a young lady answered, I announced I was a police officer, showed her my I.D., in the background I could hear someone hanging up a telephone. I went into the next room and the suspect said, he just hung up the phone from talking to a Sergeant and everything was okay. I told him everything was okay and advised he was under arrest for escaping from an Arizona Correctional Facility. I took the escapee out to the front yard of the house and the Phoenix P.D. had a patty wagon ready to transport

him to Maricopa County Jail. I followed them and submitted an arrest report.
That was called a Sergeant with a GIFT OF GAB.
A special thanks to the Phoenix P.D.

I'm Returning Your Call

John Fink #683

As a member of Air Rescue I always wondered why Officer/Paramedic Denny Welsh's missions always seemed to make it into the news. I went on some fantastic missions, saved a lot of lives, located a lot of missing persons, etc., but my missions seemed to hardly ever get noticed by the news media.
I finally figured it out. When Denny would return from a great mission he would call the media and tell them he was returning a phone call from a reporter who was asking about the call that he was just on. Of course he couldn't remember the name of the reporter. (There wasn't any reporter who had called). Whoever answered the phone would say they didn't know who had called but would go ahead and take down the information. Needless to say the mission and all its details would make it into the paper.
Got to hand it to Denny that was a classic move! He was a great medic and I do miss my friend.

The Shed

Bob Singer #2693

My first duty station was in Cameron. Eight months after getting there, ADOT finished up the new state yard in Gray Mountain north of Flagstaff. It was a 4-man duty station but most of the time, there were only 3 of us with our families there. It was up to us to get ourselves moved from the old state yard in Cameron to Gray Mountain. We each had a shed that was approximately 8'X10' and 6' high. My classmate, JD Hough, had an old International pickup truck so we decided to get the shed onto the back of the truck laying down and then I would get inside of it to weigh it down for the 10 mile trip to Gray Mountain. I guess JD got a little impatient at going slow so he started speeding up. All of a sudden, I felt the shed, with me in it, start lifting up off of the back of the truck. I started screaming for him to slow down. He apparently did hear me and slowed down with the shed clunking back down into the bed of the truck. We got safely moved to Gray Mountain.

The Prisoner Car Wash

Rich Richardson #188

One afternoon while stationed in Seligman in 1963 I decided to wash the patrol vehicle. We washed our cars at a gas station with an attached cafe. I was off duty and wearing jeans and a white t-shirt and sneakers. I finished washing the car and took a coffee break in the café. At that time I was the only customer seated at a table. I had been joking with the lady that ran the kitchen and waited tables. One of the of the gas station employees then entered the café. An idea struck me to have a bit of fun. I knew that soon some tourist would stop at the gas station for gas and possibly would enter the café for eats. I had a pair of leg irons and wrist cuffs in the patrol vehicle. I brought them into the café and chained my legs to the table stand and then put on the wrist cuffs. It didn't take too long, and a lady entered the café and sat at another table. It was obvious to the lady that I was chained to the table. I made some rattling sounds and sipped my coffee. I noticed that the tourist tried not to look my way most of the time. I asked the tourist if she'd help me tip the table so I could get my legs free. She didn't volunteer to help and tried even harder to ignore me. Eventually I slowly tipped the table on its side enough that I could slide my legs free of the base. Then I stood up and looked around. The cook was back in the kitchen at the time and the gas station attendant was taking care of a customer outside. It was just me and the tourist. I asked the tourist where she was headed. She replied Indiana. I asked if she'd give me a ride when she was ready to leave. Of course she declined the request. I walked out of the café, looked around and then got in the patrol vehicle and drove away, eastbound.

Later I was on duty and began my patrol duty. During a break, I stopped at the gas station. I heard from the gas station employee and the cook that the tourist felt sorry for me and wanted to help but was afraid to do so. She asked the gas station employee what I had done to be chained up like that. He told her that I had beat up my mother for her social security check and was in custody, doing jail time. Part of my punishment was washing the patrol car. The arresting officer had gone someplace and left the patrol vehicle unattended. The tourist left the café and headed east. The employee told me what happened after I left. He thought it was really funny and too bad that I didn't see the expressions on the tourist's face.

I gave the whole idea a lot of thought and came to the decision that this wasn't a funny joke at all. I worried all day on my shift that I might get a call from Flagstaff dispatcher to report to Flagstaff for a conference. It could have backfired on me big time. Suppose the tourists had called the sheriff's department or the patrol? I would definitely be in a lot of hot water and perhaps standing in knee deep carpet in front of G. O. Hathaway, the Superintendent. It was really a stupid thing to do. I definitely regretted what happened and would never pull such a stunt the remainder of my law enforcement career.

The Flying Budweiser Man

Steve Lump #715

Finally, as long ago promised to my long-time friend and associate, Paul ("Pep") Palmer, I am submitting this story to the fine publishing endeavor undertaken by Paul, Colin Peabody and the Coalition of DPS Retirees, a very worthwhile organization for the retired men and women of the Arizona Highway Patrol and Arizona Department of Public Safety, after a (somewhat!) brief introduction..

My name is Steve Lump, Badge #715 and I served and retired from that fine outfit, serving as a cadet-officer dispatcher/op comm (phone/teletype/NLETS) operator, highway patrolman (trooper), ALEOAC instructor (First Responder/EMS/EMT/American Red Cross-First Aid certification) paramedic-officer, motor-officer and agent/ detective, along with 9 yrs. as AHPA (ASTA) president and NTC 1st VP, all between April 16, 1970 and May 31, 1991, a career of several "firsts" and "lasts" of which I am obviously proud.

My issued badge number upon hire, in-between cadet/academy classes in 1970 was Badge #123, possibly issued for its simplicity and ease of remembrance(?) and it changed to Badge #715 January 1, 1972, at 0001Hrs. (I was out there, working). I started my career as one of the last "commissioned cadet/officer candidates" hired under an old program requiring 2 years of op-comm commitment, before academy or HP duty assignment. As a stroke of good luck, that changed and ended shortly afterwards, and I was sent to the academy, Cadet Class #16, in August 1970.

My first duty posting out of the academy, was likely the last outpost (remote duty station) DPS ever created (?), when I was assigned to the newly opening Bullhead City 2-man duty station, due to the State's extension of SR95 from I-40, Topock and Needles, CA, to Davis Dam and SR68, in District 1. I spent the first year and a half out there (over the hills, on the Colorado river) by my lonesome, while the Southern California Edison coal slurry-fired electric generation plant was being built in Laughlin, NV, by Bechtel Corp. with approximately 2500 contracted construction tradesmen (boilermakers, ironworkers-welders, carpenters, electricians, you get the point!), all living in every available space in the area, and on union subsistence, **with** four (4, count em') 24-hour a day casinos operating right next to them, cashing their paychecks for free and free adult beverages with gambling to drive pass twice a day.. mayhem was ensuing! "Oh, the Overtime!", as we used to say, when comp-time (only) was accrued at an hour for an hour, for all overtime.

Yup… back in the day! (And, that's as brief as I can usually be..!)

After a fairly brief time in my first (read: "Rookie") duty station posting, and still the only officer at what was supposed to be a 2-man Remote Duty Station, Bullhead City (BHC), a delightfully temperate garden spot, along the Colorado River with summertime, daytime temperatures averaging near 120 degrees, river gnats so thick they appeared as clouds, and every local knowing what the "Bullhead City Wave" was (one hand always held high above your head to attract the gnats to that point!) I was literally working my tail off, working mostly swing shifts (at my request, due to drunk construction workers, crashes, etc.)

One evening, late after booking my second DWI (that's what we called them back in early 70's with .15 BAC the law of the land and Mobat (balloon field tests) being the confirmation method, aside from anyone at .15 BAC and above being unable to pass <u>any</u> of the "sobriety" field tests, and those DWI arrests each requiring my driving from somewhere near my BHC area, to downtown Kingman and Mohave County's Jail each and every time. (Early in the new area I booked nearly every DUI driver I arrested, as an enforcement model attempting to reduce the problem, with the local population hopefully coming to realize, "Drive drunk, go to jail" in Kingman!)

On my second return trip west, back to my area (BHC) from Kingman, and just passing over the crest of the Black Mountains on SR68, I encountered an old VW Bus eastbound and with a single male driver, across the centerline, mostly in my westbound lane. The area requires some strategic planning just to turn around due to the steep mountainous down grade, curves and such, but was quickly accomplished and the chase was on! The eastbound downgrade is no less steep and the VW Bus, though slightly under the posted limit was ALL OVER THE ROAD (again, it was only a 2 lane highway from Davis Dam on The Colorado River to the junction of US93 and the Kingman Port of entry, excluding some passing lanes through the mountainous area.

(A slight confession is required here: It was late and going to be another justified, but not sought-after, long overtime shift and it was still hot outside. I was tiring of drunk drivers filling many of my waking hours, plus hour-for-hour O/T, only accrued on the books (not paid!), and this was certainly going to necessitate another trip to the jail in Kingman, and I was also sure those jailers were tired of seeing me! Plus, another late 10-7, missed dinner, etc.)

As the VW Bus wandered over both lanes I “lit it up” with top mount emergency lights, my wig-wag head lights and after no response, my siren. The VW Bus then crossed over again completely into the W/B lanes, over-corrected, crossing back into the E/B lane, off onto the shoulder, over-correcting again and began to slide sideways dancing on the right wheels only and began to roll over. As the vehicle was violently beginning to roll onto it's top, while traveling broadside, the driver's door sprang open and the (very drunk) driver came sailing out, high into the air, followed immediately by somewhere near a case or more of mostly empty Budweiser beer cans, almost as if they were a tail, tied to a kite (said driver) and followed him airborne, as he sailed towards and onto the westbound shoulder, landing awkwardly and face down, with a severe thud and a cloud of dust, with all those beer cans then following him and landing on and all around him. Such a sight, I had never even contemplated seeing. The VW bus rolled (flipping) two and one half times, also landing in the westbound shoulder, but somehow missing the "Flying Budweiser Man" and landing upside down and coming to rest somewhere close, but past him.

I immediately called (radioed) the accident in and was certain I had witnessed what would be a fatal accident (Code 963 X1) and a brilliant thought then occurred to me! Heck, I'm a witness and Flagstaff (our nighttime dispatching service) should call someone else out to handle this accident, as I am the sole witness, so, I suggested the same to my Flagstaff dispatcher.. I then quickly (we always act quickly and professionally) got out of my patrol car and ran up to confirm that the driver was no longer amongst the living. Shaking him and beginning to check for a pulse, He woke up, spitting out some teeth and dirt, and said: "Well, shit". To which, obviously being further startled, I responded: "Yes sir, that would perfectly some up what just happened!" Next Flagstaff radio advised me (in no uncertain terms) that per some unnamed supervisor (probably mine, now also advised of the situation), told radio to inform me that the accident, drunk arrest, etc. were all mine to sort out and handle (not a surprise, albeit disappointing that my reasoning was in error!) Nice try!

Surprisingly (to me at that early stage in my career) the driver/drunk/victim was only minorly injured for the most part, as it turned out, so after an ambulance ride to the Kingman hospital, a tow truck, accident investigation and whatnot, I eventually proceeded to the hospital, where the driver was treated and released (still a truism: drunks come out way too good and lucky, injury-wise in wrecks!), arrested and booked (#3 that shift) into the Mohave County jail, and I had another accident report, arrest report, tow truck inventory, blah, blah) to add to that week's paperwork. (And weekly Recap, don't you know? "Eight a day keep the Sergeant away...!"

I can say now, all my memories of that assignment to D-1 as the first Highway Patrol

Officer in Bullhead City are very and sincerely fondly remembered.

Good Samaritans

Daryl Mullins #480

It was the summer of 1968; I had been out of the academy for a couple of months and was stationed 37 miles west of Kingman on US 66 at a state yard called Franconia Wash with a seasoned patrolman and his family. Patrolman Dick North and his family lived in a small house and myself and my family lived in a 12x60 mobile home.

I was off duty one evening and received a call from dispatch advising there was a three car accident six miles east of the California State line. I got my uniform on, jumped in my patrol car and headed west on US66. About a mile and a half before I got to the accident site traffic was stopped and there was no traffic coming eastbound. The area where the accident was located was a mountain pass that dropped off on both sides of the highway so there was no place for the vehicles to go around. The accident vehicles were placed in the road and the damage was such they could not be readily moved. The injuries were minor except one of the passengers in one of the vehicles had a heart attack. There was a nurse in one of the stopped cars that assisted with the heart attack victim. It was a dead communication area so I had no contact to get assistance. I got some truck drivers together and we were able to bounce and move two of the cars enough to open a space large enough to get cars through. I asked some drivers of the moving cars to contact Kingman dispatch to have an ambulance come from Needles, Calif. and three wreckers from Kingman. 5 hours later I was on my way to Needles to do follow up.

I finished up at the Needles hospital and found that the heart attack victim was going to be fine. Thank goodness for the nurse and the truck drivers.

Sleeping With The Mayor?

Louie Chaboya #1139

Sergeant Roger Illingsworth was Harold Swyers #3424 (May he rest in peace) and my Sergeant when the two of us were assigned to narcotics in Nogales. The three of us were in the office one day doing reports. Harold was in one room, and I was with Sergeant Illingsworth in another. Sergeant Illingsworth was asking me how Harold was performing. I advised that Harold and I were getting along quite well except that I was a little concerned about Harrold in that I found out that he was sleeping with the Mayor of Patagonia. Sergeant Illingsworth got quite upset and yelled at Harold to come into his office. "What is this that I hear that you are sleeping with the Mayor of

Patagonia" he yelled at Harold. "Yes I am. Is that a problem with you?" Harold asked.

"Absolutely it is. What if your wife finds out" Sergeant Illingsworth asked?

Harold's reply: "Well, my wife is the Mayor"

Guess who Sergeant Illingsworth then started yelling at? No, I did not get any punishment other than being yelled at.

A Great Team

Lee Patterson #2733

While recently looking through some vintage Arizona Department of Public Safety (DPS) Digest issues I had saved over the years, I came across a past issue published in 1984 and after seeing it again, it evoked a flood of memories. The digest article was entitled "Officers report positive results with marriages". It went on to state "Officers married to officers. They face danger. They share common experiences. They worry about each other, but not as much as some might think, since they have confidence in each other's skills".

A few married DPS sworn officer couples were featured in the article including my wife Cindy and me. Back then it wasn't the norm to have that many married couples serving together on the department. In those days I was a Highway Patrol uniformed motorcycle officer and motor training instructor working the metro Phoenix freeways, also referred to by us as “the ditch”. I was living the dream as they say, as my career goal at that point was to remain on motors until I retired. That would later completely change for me. Cindy was also then assigned to the Phoenix metro Highway Patrol Bureau (HPB) as a uniformed officer working in a car squad. She was a very accomplished and efficient officer and considered an exceptional Trooper by her supervisors and peers. As a result, my concerns for her safety were alleviated somewhat, although I still had the typical worries any loving husband would have, and I know Cindy felt the same about my abilities and welfare on the job as well.

Our lifestyle was generally atypical compared to what most married men and women experienced during the course of their marriages. We embraced our career choices in that regard however, and we were very happy together. We had many memorable on-duty “married cop” moments together back in the proverbial good old days of our careers. A brief overview of our more interesting on-the-job events follows.

The department was always very accommodating with our married status by allowing us to work in the same district and on similar shifts. We frequently responded jointly to calls and worked well as a team. As it was alluded to in the digest article, we knew each other’s reactions and handled stressful tactical enforcement scenarios well together. On several occasions when we had court cases scheduled simultaneously, we sat together in the courtroom until called to testify with our respective cases by the bailiffs. When our last name was called, we would both stand up, which always got a chuckle from the presiding judges and other officers waiting to testify.

In 1983, we were assigned to work Morenci mine strike duty during the course of the strike's evolution. Since we and some of the other married officer couples involved didn't have any children, we all volunteered to work the assignment during Christmas week so the other officers in the department with kids could remain at home with them during the holidays. When Cindy and I checked into the local motel, the desk clerk thought it was a terribly funny joke when we told her we wanted a room together. The clerk wouldn't give us a room until we showed ID proving we had the same last names and residence address and were in fact married! We also shared a patrol car together on that assignment and in a symbolic holiday gesture, we hung a little Christmas ornament from Cindy's radio microphone bracket in her patrol car.

On another night in 1983, Cindy and I assisted in delivering a baby girl in the front seat of a car parked in the emergency lane on one of the Phoenix freeways. We also worked a number of traffic accident investigations throughout the course of our shifts in "the ditch" together as well.

During the monsoons, a number of the freeway underpasses flooded. If swing cars weren't available, I would park my motor and patrol with Cindy until the end of our shifts, and there were many times when we found ourselves "floating" in her patrol car as we rescued stranded motorists.

In 1984, only three years after she had completed the DPS Police academy, Cindy became one of the first two women in departmental history to promote to the rank of Sergeant. I certainly hadn't ever previously had any desire to ever kiss a Sergeant, but I do believe I may have been the first Arizona State Trooper to have done so, when I gave "Sgt. Cindy" a big congratulatory kiss on the lips for her well-earned promotion!

In 1985, while on vacation in Great Britain, we were given the red carpet treatment in the United Kingdom (UK) by the Metropolitan Police Department. Cindy was the DPS sworn selection supervisor at the time, and had made arrangements through official channels to meet with her counterparts at the "Met" headquarters in London in order to compare recruitment programs and respective police candidate selection methodologies. Since I was then an active motorcycle officer and instructor, and had been involved with evaluations of motor officer equipment and motorcycle assessments for possible departmental fleet acquisition, arrangements were also made for me to meet with the "Met" motorcycle program staff as well. We were given full access to areas and information seldom made available to the public. We both were able to bring back valuable procedural and operational information which was subsequently disseminated to DPS. We were also allowed to patrol with a police boat crew on the Thames river and we inspected the Met's motorcycle and automotive facilities to include driving on their emergency vehicle operator training track. We were even driven to the Prime Minister's residence at number 10 Downing Street which obviously wasn't open to public access. In addition we were shown their police academy at Hendon and toured their "Black" museum located at the New Scotland Yard facility. Interestingly, the "Bobbies" were seemingly fascinated with American cops and found it somewhat unusual that we were actually allowed to work together on the job as a married couple. The whole "UK" experience was obviously not what a typical married couple does while on vacation, but we absolutely loved it!

In 1988, Cindy also became the first women at DPS to promote to the rank of Lieutenant. By then, I had left my HPB motor assignment and was serving as a plain-clothed Criminal Investigations Bureau (CIB) detective in the Special Investigations Unit (SIU) where I remained until my retirement in 2000. In 1992, Cindy unfortunately had to take a medical retirement due to a prior on-duty back injury, ending a relatively short but very promising law enforcement career.

At the time of her retirement, Cindy was a District Commander, and again was the first women in DPS history to hold such responsibilities. I was then and will always be so proud of Cindy not only as a loving husband but also as a fellow State Trooper.

Cindy subsequently endured several major back surgeries following her retirement, and was later diagnosed with breast cancer. Following intense treatment for her cancer diagnosis, she was eventually deemed cancer free, but five years later it came back with a vengeance. In 2012, Cindy passed away following a lengthy battle when the cancer metastasized and spread to her bones. She fought it gallantly with tough determination, elegance, grace, and dignity….just as she had always conducted herself while serving as a State Trooper who had been happily married to another State Trooper. Hopefully the aforementioned chronology adequately has described how two married cops had experienced life in the Arizona DPS, the greatest law enforcement agency in the world.

Daddy, Daddy, Daddy!

Roger Vanderpool #2694

I was the CI Sgt in Casa Grande and our squad was doing a search warrant on a home in Eloy along with the Pinal County Narcotics Task Force. The house at the time the warrant was served was occupied by three females, one being in her thirties, then a teenage female about 15 or 16 and her 3 year old little girl. When we entered and separated everyone, they said they only spoke Spanish, so we called one of our Spanish speaking officers, Miguel Renteria 2734 in to interview them. As soon as Miguel entered the room and the toddler saw him she immediately ran over to him and hugged his leg screaming Daddy, Daddy, Daddy. I thought Miguel was going to pass out. All the officers in the room turned and looked at him, (Miguel is married) knowing that obviously whoever the father was had committed a crime by having sex with the young girl. Miguel began stammering, Roger I have never seen this girl in my life, I'm not the father.

Pinal County Sheriff's Office Sgt Dave Harrington, turned to Miguel and said I guess this goes from a narcotics case to a sex crime case. Miguel about passed out. For about a week afterward we had a lot of laughs at Miguel's expense telling him Professional Standards was going to be contacting him.

The SO never did figure out who the father was, but it wasn't Miguel.

False Arrest

Richard Richardson #188

Friday, May 28, 1965 in the Show Low area was very warm. I recall that day I was on regular patrol duty working the afternoon/evening shift on US 60, less than three miles west of the community city limits. As best I can recall, it may have been about 1830 and the sun was getting ready to reach the western horizon. US 60, was a paved 30 foot curvy two lane highway with no emergency parking area on either edge of the pavement. There was about a four foot sloping berm on each side of the paved portion and a thick number of Ponderosa Pine trees on both sides of the roadway.

The near setting sun and tree shadows resulted in poor visibility for motorists to see a pedestrian walking along side of the road in either direction making it not a good place for anyone driving to attempt to stop and pick up anyone hitchhiking. I noticed a hitch hiker walking toward town and with the eastbound traffic flow behind him. Hitchhiking is against the law in the state, but is loosely applied by officers. I believed the situation could prove to be dangerous for the hitchhiker as well as anyone attempting to pick him up. Traffic was not too heavy at the time, but still dangerous. I did see his thumb motioning to vehicles as a hitchhiker usually does.

I made an emergency stop and questioned the hitchhiker. He didn't see anything wrong in what he was doing and that he wasn't hitchhiking. I asked about if he carried any money and he claimed he had none. His attitude was not good. All I could do at the time was issue him a traffic ticket for hitchhiking and let him go. I knew that he would continue to hitchhike after I left. I made a decision for his safety and the fact that he claimed not to have any money. I arrested him as a vagrant. We could do that at the time. The vagrancy law in Arizona at the time was a good charge enabling me to take him into custody.

The Navajo County Sheriff's department maintained a non-attended jail facility during those days in Show Low. That meant there were no jailers on duty at the facility. The two cells did have a toilet and wash basin along with a fixed cot. I took him to Show Low and placed him in a holding cell. The procedure was to notify my AHP Holbrook dispatcher that I placed a prisoner in the temporary holding facility. It was the charge of the dispatcher to notify the sheriff's department about a prisoner being held in the Show Low facility. A local deputy would take over the care of a prisoner. I continued patrolling the highways until my shift concluded. I didn't think any more about the man in the Show Low jail.

Saturday, Sunday and Monday passed by as I patrolled the highways. Sunday was Memorial

Day. I never gave any thought about the prisoner, assuming that he probably was released or transported to the main Navajo County jail in Holbrook. The sheriff's department would have contacted either the County Attorney or a judge concerning the prisoner and any bail that might be set. What I didn't know was the deputy residing in Show Low never got the message about the prisoner. Of course I didn't know that either. Tuesday was my one day off. The patrol in those days, an officer worked six days a week and nine hours each day, unless an emergency arose and overtime would be needed.

I received a telephone call from the AHP dispatcher in Holbrook during Tuesday morning that I was to report to the holding jail in Show Low immediately. I didn't know what the reason was. I put on my uniform quickly and drove to Show Low. The deputy on duty was at the holding jail. He advised me that he discovered the prisoner that morning while making a routine stop at the jail facility to do some paper work. He discovered the prisoner at that time. The poor guy was in the facility all this time without any deputy knowing about the man. Whoever dropped the communication ball? I don't know and never found out. The deputy advised that I take the prisoner to Pinetop and have Judge F.E Thomas hear the case immediately, of which I concurred.

The prisoner was happy that I arrived and would take him to court and was very hungry. We arrived in Pinetop. The judge was in his office. I spoke privately with the judge and informed him of the situation. The judge was agreeable and decided that he'd see if the man would plead guilty, he'd pronounce a sentence of five days in jail, credit for time served and a hundred dollar suspended fine. The man could be released from custody immediately. In those days, if a person could hire an attorney and there weren't any appointed attorney by the court in misdemeanors. The judge asked if the man could afford an attorney. Of course the prisoner responded he didn't have money. We both worried about if the man pleads not guilty and request a trial. We both knew that the man had a possible case of false arrest if he talked to an attorney and there just might be a law suit over the arrest due to the extenuating circumstances of the incarceration. The prisoner then went before the judge and was advised of his pleas. In those days there wasn't any 'Miranda ' rights given to prisoners. The Ernesto Miranda rights hadn't happened yet. The prisoner did enter a plea of guilty. Judge Thomas was happy and pronounced sentence. The prisoner was happy to be released from custody.

Now there was still a problem. What was the man going to do in Pinetop? He was still without money and on foot. I offered to take him to Show

Low and he accepted. At least he'd be almost back to where he would have been if he'd had not been arrested. His attitude was cordial, not like before. I believe that he was just happy not to have still been in that jail. I drove him to Show Low and we stopped at the White Mountain Café near the junction of US 60 and SR 77. I advised the man that he could have any breakfast he wanted to order, paid by me. He thought that was really nice. He did in fact order a good breakfast and enjoyed several cups of coffee. I asked him what his destination was. He advised that he was heading to Oklahoma. I then advised him about hitchhiking as being illegal in most states and if an officer wanted to enforce a law, the man could be in a similar situation again. I suggested that he not select dangerous places to try and hitch rides, that way the chances of his being arrested would be less. He agreed with me. I decided to drive him to Holbrook. I suggested that perhaps he ask for rides at one of the truck stops and maybe he'd have a better chance of getting to Oklahoma. He agreed and I drove him to Holbrook and left him off at a truck stop on US 66 that had a café attached. I gave him a twenty dollar bill and recommended that he hold onto some of that money so he wouldn't be called a vagrant again. He actually thanked me and shook my hand. I left the area and didn't look back. I hoped that he wouldn't ever press the five days spent at the Show Low's holding jail. I never heard anything from him and no law suit for false arrest.

I did advise Sgt. Ray Dahm (AHP 708) of the incident. He said it wasn't necessary to submit an 'Incident Report 'since there was a record of the arrest and the courts outcome. He did advise that I did the right thing in handling the case as it was handled. I really believed that he may have worried a bit about a possible lawsuit someday, that never happened.

What I learned from that arrest was to check on any prisoner welfare that I would lock up at that or any other non-attending holding jail. It wasn't too long afterwards that all county non-attended jails were stopped from being used. There would have to be a 24 hour jailers available for all prisoners locked up in any county jail in the state.

Talk To My Sergeant

John Fink #683

While speeding into work at the Tucson Airport where DPS housed our Air Rescue Helicopter, I noticed someone following me the last few miles. I pulled into the parking lot and this individual pulled right in behind me and asked if I was a cop. I stated I was, and he said he had been following me and started yelling at me about my speeding. At that time my Sergeant Sam Fragala happened to be coming out of the hanger and I said to this individual - here's my sergeant - talk to him - and I went inside the hanger.

After a few minutes Sam came back into the hanger. I was getting ready for a you know what chewing out and a PPR entry but all Sam said to me was "Fink - knock it off!"

I respected Sam for that and needless to say that was the last time I sped coming into work - NOT!

Testy Sports Figures

Ron Bruce #2048

I was working off-duty highway construction traffic control on Interstate 40, east of Flagstaff in the mid 1990's as I recall. The construction crew was complaining of speeders in the speed reduction zone and we were working to try and slow folks down. I had a speeder doing 75 in the 45 reduction zone and made a traffic stop. The vehicle as I recall was a Cadillac. The driver was accompanied by his wife in the right front seat. The white male driver was immediately hostile. After getting his paperwork, I realized he was Major League Baseball player and manager, Dick Williams (Richard Hirschfeld Williams). Williams had been a somewhat average major league player but played from 1951 to 1964. He then ultimately worked as a major league manager for the Boston Red Sox, Oakland Athletics, California Angels, Montreal Expos, San Diego Padres and Seattle

Mariners over a span through 1988. He was inducted into the Hall of Fame in 2008. He managed teams to four World Series and won two of those.

As I was trying to explain the reason for the stop, which Williams knew before I even walked up to his vehicle, he yelled at me, “Yeah, yeah, yeah, just write the f- -king ticket buddy!” From body language, it was obvious his wife was mortified.

Now, Williams “enjoyed” a reputation as not getting along well with umpires. In fact, he was largely despised by umpiring crews. I finished the citation and re-contacted Williams. Attempting to explain his options in dealing with the citation, he again yelled at me and said, “Look, just give it here so I can sign the S.O.B.”

I handed the clipboard to his wife who passed it to her husband. She glanced up at me and her eyes were saying how sorry she was. I understood. Getting the clipboard back and tearing off Williams ’copy, I handed it in along with the standard (by then) court envelope with instructions. I leaned further down and looking at Williams I said, “Mr. Williams, I’m getting a really good idea why umpires hated you so much!” I thought his wife was going to choke from laughing. Williams just gave off a loud grunt and drove away.

In the early 1980s, while working traffic on Interstate 10, I made a traffic stop on an eastbound new Buick Rivera for 75 in the maximum speed limit zone of 55. This was in the area of milepost 197. On approaching the driver's side of the vehicle (we were not yet doing right side approaches) I immediately recognized the driver as Paul Westphal, an NBA player who I had seen play for the Phoenix Suns and by then had been traded to the Seattle Supersonics. Westphal ultimately played for five NBA teams and also coached for five NBA teams, as well as three college teams.

I explained the reason for the stop, which Westphal seemed to take in stride. He had what appeared to be three African-American basketball players with him. Finishing the citation and re-contacting Westphal, knowing full well who he was and what he did for a living, I asked him, "Sir, if you are employed, who do you work for?", as the citation asked for that information. He responded, "You've got to be kidding, right? I play basketball for the Supersonics." As I was writing that information down, one of his passengers snorted and said, "Hell Paul, he must be a baseball fan!" Mr. Westphal signed the citation and went on his way.

I Could Have Strangled Him

Dick Lewis #176

One Fourth of July weekend Sgt Jim Snedigar was riding with me, and we were driving through the Salt River Canyon. When we approached the bridge at the bottom of the canyon, there was a woman standing at the railing of the bridge waving her arms. We stopped and she told us there was a small girl in the river.

Jim and I climbed down under the bridge to a point that was a sheer drop off with the river about 100 feet below. We could see a man beside the river giving mouth to mouth resuscitation to a small child.

Some college students were on the other side of the river and hollered, "Hey take off your gun belt and dive in". Ignoring them we made our way to a spot where we could get closer to the river. When we got close, we hollered to the man to bring the child to us.

I took the child in my arms and began running to my patrol car as Jim continued to give the girl mouth to mouth. Jim jumped in the back seat with the child, continuing mouth to mouth. Jim said, "I think she's dead." I told him that yes, she was. I could just tell.

We stopped and picked up the girl's mother and father and headed to Globe which was 35 miles away, code 3. Jim continued mouth to mouth all the way to Globe. We maneuvered through the

Fourth of July traffic and got to Globe in record time. By the time we arrived at the hospital, my brakes were gone.

The girl was pronounced dead at the hospital. The mother was standing in the hallway sobbing and the father who was intoxicated told her, "Don't cry, we have four more children." I could have strangled him!

(Note: Jim and I were advised of a complaint filed by those college students. We never were told what the complaint was. Director Hegarty wrote it off as drunk college students and nothing ever came of it. Guess they thought we should have dived into the river.)

You're Hired

Gay Anderson #813

In Sept of 1970 I was just starting my sophomore year at Arizona Western College in Yuma, majoring in law enforcement. The instructor had set up a program where the students rode one shift a week with Highway Patrolmen. Excerpt for me - no females were allowed in patrol cars and there were no female officers. So I was assigned to radio where 3 of the dispatchers were officers who were assigned right out of the academy. I took to it like a duck to water.

By the time Christmas came around I worked 2 weeks all by myself. Not that there was much there - a radio console and a teletype machine on which

I could run a 10-29. For 27's or 28's I had to call MVD or DDl.in Phx where they had college students working. The integrity of the return depended on the work ethic of the college student. Something we had to call Phx Security to go wake them up. If you wanted a 27 or 28 from out of state, I had to send a teletype and it would take a couple days for a return.

Unknown to me, the District Commander had suggested that since they were talking about completely civilianizing radio he had a good candidate. On April 16, 1971 I went in, took my written test, my typing test and oral board. I was immediately hired and started work at 1600 that afternoon. I went to Phx the next week to do paperwork and get my uniform - white blouse and brown skirt. I was classified as a communications equipment operator and my badge number was 6135. When we changed badge numbers, I became 813. This last June I attended the grand reopening of Tucson OpComm and I was flabbergasted and awestruck by the technology now available.

Too Smart For His Own Good

Don Barcello #515

I was working in Phoenix communications in the early 70’s when communications got its first computers. Lt George Elias (RIP) was our lieutenant.

Everyone was experimenting with the new system and was sending messages back and forth to each other. Patrolman Roger Waters (RIP) was also assigned to communications, and he decided to send me a message. Thinking he was sending to me only, he typed in Don Barcello is a s—t hyphen head. He mistakenly hit a wrong button and the message went to the entire department.

It wasn't long before one of the ladies in the business office called Lt Elias and told him about the message everyone in the business office had received. That was the first call, and then Lt Elias began getting many more complaints calls.

The lieutenant had to get to the bottom of this quickly. He talked to every single person assigned to communications and would ask each person how to spell s—t head. Everyone spelled out s—t head. Except Roger. When Lt Elias asked him how to spell s—t head, without hesitation, he responded s—t hyphen head. Gotcha the lieutenant said. Not sure if Roger was disciplined for that or not.

Old School vs New

Dennis McNulty #1959

I was a dispatcher in Phoenix opcomm from 1976 to 1981. We had the first-generation cathode-ray type style computer displays, but we also had a teletype machine with a keyboard and a ticker tape printer that was part of the NLETS (National Law

Enforcement Teletype System). This was the system that allowed police departments nationwide to send messages to each other. I'm not sure why its computers were here at DPS but they were. There was an NLETS person who took care of it during day shift, but folks on swing and graveyard shifts had to keep an eye on it. We were shown some basic things to do.

Each winter the police department in Buffalo, New York, which gets a lot of snow, would perversely send out a very long detailed message specifically explaining exactly how much snow they had and a list of how many local roads and highways that were closed. Invariably this long message would jam up the NLETS computers for everyone else.

Whoever was out in the opcomm phone center would have to go out to switch the NLETS computer over to the teletype machine and use the ticker tape printer to physically pull that message out of the system, which would give us about 50-60 feet of ticker tape.

Old system keeping the new system going!

Computer Art

Paul Palmer #342

I remember those long teletypes Dennis talked about. I first saw them when I was dispatching in Holbrook and hated getting them. No problem if you weren't busy, but if you had messages to send, your work got tied up until those long messages ended. Phoenix did wait to send those out until the graveyard shift.

When I got to Phoenix, I observed what Dennis talks about. I never saw the message from Buffalo but at Christmas time someone would send a messages made up X's and O's that would form a picture. It would be a Christmas tree or winter scene. I forget who sent them but it must have taken days to put the images together. They sometimes would be 3 or more feet long and we would put a tall trash basket by the machine to catch the ticker tape to keep people from walking all over it.

Another favorite was from Texas. If the Longhorns won the National football title you could count on getting a huge image of a Longhorn coming across the system. It would take forever to finish coming in.

The Morning Report

Ralph Shartzer #220

It was around 1970 and I was working in Phoenix communications while I attended Phoenix College. Each morning at 6:00 on a dedicated line, Bill Heywood with radio station KTAR would call for a live morning report. We would have it all typed up with information on fatalities, accident statistics and other items of interest.

One morning I was sitting in the large teletype room waiting for the call. Everyone had left the room so that it would be quiet for the call. The phone rang and I answered it, "Good morning, Ralph Shartzer, Arizona Highway Patrol". Instead of hearing Bill Heywood's voice I heard a frantic woman saying that her house was being broken into. I'm thinking, how in the heck did this woman get this phone number. This was before there was a 911 number.

She was whispering a lot, hiding in a closet. I looked around and there is no one to help me. I tried to get her location and found out that she was in Mesa. I maneuvered found and managed to pick another nearby phone and called Mesa PD. I am juggling two phones, one in each ear and trying to dial the second phone as I tried to get her address and give the information to Mesa PD. I must have looked like a contortionist in a side show.

I finally got the address and then stayed on the line until Mesa PD arrived at her address. It all worked out to the good, but I sure could have used an extra arm. Or maybe just some help.

I don't recall if Bill Heywood ever called that morning or not.

A-10 Air Strike?

Gay Anderson #813

The prelude to this story is the incident in Kingman in 1973 when the tanker train blevied and killed a lot of firemen and Patrolman Allen Hanson.

In 1975 or 1976 I was the supervisor on day shift in Phx Radio. My dispatcher called me to come listen to a recording of a transmission. There had been a train derailment with propane tanks in the western part of the state. There were no leaks or problems. A fairly new sgt told my dispatcher to call Luke AFB and order up an A-10 airstrike to prevent a bigger problem.
Well I picked up the phone, but I didn't call Luke, I called Col Milldebrandt, who knew exactly what to say. I can just imagine calling Luke "Hi this is the Highway Patrol and I need an A-10 strike to destroy a Southern Pacific train." Yeah right.

Unsung Heroes

Paul Palmer #342

Unsung heroes is a term that describes the department's dispatchers. I say this not because I was a dispatcher but because I know what a demanding and critical job it is.
I have no concept of what current DPS dispatchers deal with. Their work is much different than the world of dispatching I knew in 1966. So bear with this old man as I recall the old days.
After returning to Arizona after four years in the Navy, I hired on as a dispatcher with the Arizona Highway Patrol on April 1st, 1966, in Holbrook

making $432.00 a month. More money that I had ever made before in my life.

At the time there were communications centers in Kingman, Flagstaff, Holbrook, Yuma, Phoenix, Claypool, Tucson and Nogales.

Male dispatchers wore the highway patrol uniform, without gun belt of course. Over the left shirt pocket we wore a small black patch with the word "Communications" in gold stitching. The female dispatchers wore a white blouse and brown skirt.

The radio console had a flat metal face with a swivel boom mic and toggle switches for each frequency. We had a phone with a local line, a microwave line and a hot line to the PD and SO. We had a civil defense phone and speaker box that would run civil defense phone tests several times a day. They would call and you would respond with "Holbrook Highway Patrol". You would hear the roll call of the entire state. The sheriff's offices throughout the state were also on this link. You would hear each station respond. The sheriff's offices also used this to link with patrol offices. The most frequently heard was "Bisbee SO to Nogales patrol." I always wondered if they had phones in Bisbee.

You had a handwritten log to record every call from the patrolmen. It was required that you wrote the patrolman's entire message verbatim. This got difficult during winter snowstorms or during the summer vacation months when horrific fatalities occurred. You could tell how busy your shift was by the number of hand log pages at the end of your shift. Since you had to have the entire conversation, you would be writing furiously as the patrolmen called in for 27's, 28's and 29's. They would also call in their accident reports that you would then have to type on the daily log. I remember one graveyard shift HP35 Tom Greenwade called in and I began writing as he spoke. "HP35 I am at the scene of a 963, car/frog." I finished writing the word frog as he spoke it. Now what? You couldn't alter the log. It remained.

You had no help. It was you, the patrolman, phones, walk in traffic and the dreaded teletype machine. The machine from hell. All patrol communications centers were linked together on this particular line. We received APB's, ATL's, stolen vehicles and weather condition reports. If the machine was quiet it meant is was ok for you to send a message. Too many times, you would be sending lengthy fatality reports to Phoenix and get interrupted by a radio call, phone call, or foot traffic in the lobby. You may be in the middle of the report and another station not hearing any typing going on, would jump in and start typing a message. That killed your report, and you would have to start all over from the beginning. A few curse words were uttered at those times.

During snowstorms it got extremely chaotic. Patrolmen running from accident to accident, phones that wouldn't stop ringing and people lined up in the lobby to ask road conditions. If this wasn't enough, Phoenix would ask for a road and weather report. I knew it was important to Phoenix, but to me, it was another request that I just didn't need. I always laughed because you knew that Flagstaff would report snow packed and icy roads for a 30-mile radius. Each road in the district was always reported with the same conditions each time. Only when they weren't too busy would you see change in their road conditions.

The days before NCIC and NLETS you would have to call Phoenix to get an out of state 10-27, 10-28 or 10-29.

This was time consuming and at times would take hours.

You could get 10-29's faster because Gracie Bertch in Phoenix handled to Auto Status line and would call California and also check the Phoenix card index.

When Phoenix sent APB's and stolen vehicles they were typed onto the daily log and once each shift the units were told to stand by for wanted vehicle summary. After making certain there was no more traffic coming in, you would begin to broadcast the information. We also had to identify the towers every hour. This was before the automatic identifiers.

Those were the good ole days. In my humble opinion it was a mistake to close all the outlying communications centers. The people in those centers knew their areas like the back of their hands. They were given tours of the district prior to sitting down at a console. They were known by people who had dealings with the patrol. They were not just some detached voice. It was not fair to the dispatchers in Phoenix. They got a heavier work load with an area they were not familiar with. As an example, one early morning I was covering the supervisors desk in Phoenix when a dispatcher said they had a report of a bad 962 at Pacific U on US60. An ambulance was needed. When I asked further, they said they thought it was in the Apache Junction area, but the officers there had never heard of it. I asked who had called it in and she said it was the highway department. Having been stationed in Holbrook, I immediately knew where it was. I told the dispatcher it was Cibicue on US60 at the far north end of the district they were working. They then dispatched an officer and an ambulance.

I am not being critical of dispatchers in Phoenix. I also worked in the Phoenix center. It was at times busy, chaotic and hectic. I just hated to see the outlaying stations close. But that was a decision made by people above my pay grade who had more information that I had.

Johnny Walker

Gay Anderson #813

On Nov 30, 1979, I was the supervisor in Tucson radio on swing shift. We only had two radio consoles, one for District 8 and one for District 9 and CI. At that time there was no secure channel for CI so if they were on a surveillance we could hear everything that was going on. It was a quiet night and CI was working a buy/bust at the Tucson airport, where Johnny Walker was making the buy. All of a sudden Jack Johnson came on the radio and said "Hey guys I think John's been smoked. John's been smoked." My dispatcher looked at me and asked, "Does that mean his cover has been blown?" My response was "No it means he's been shot." Then all hell broke loose. It has been 43 years and I can still hear that as clear as day. My 31 years in radio were wonderful. I had a lot of great, fun times. Unfortunately all too often there were days like Nov 30, 1979. RIP Johnny.

Who Said That?

Paul Palmer #342

One evening I was working radio in Holbrook. Everyone had gone for the day and the parking lot was empty except for a few Highway Department vehicles. The patrol shared a building with the Highway Department at the time. The maintenance radios had been handed over to me as the employees next door were getting ready to go home.

It was snowing down in Show Low, and I was pretty busy. A snow plow driver down in Show Low called in and was asking for information. I explained that the maintenance people had left for the day and he was talking to the Highway Patrol dispatcher and I was unable to get the information that he wanted. He could not grasp the fact that he was not talking to the maintenance dispatcher and kept requesting the information.

I was getting calls from patrolmen, and the phone would not quit ringing. I was losing my patience. I eased my foot off the transmit pedal to the halfway position which
was mute and I began to turn the room blue with my tirade. I questioned the plow drivers intelligence and heritage among other things.

The intercom from the Highway Department rang and it was Eleanore Smith, a friend and former patrol dispatcher. She asked who was cursing over the radio. The district engineer was in the office she said and he was extremely irate and wanted to know who in the world was cursing. I promised her I would look into it.

Eleanor whispered, I recognize your voice Paul.

I later learned that when you used the mute function, everything you said went out over the speakers over in the highway department office.

The identity of the person loudly venting profanity was never revealed. It was Eleanor's and my secret.

The Tie

Don Barcello #515

I was working in Phoenix communications, waiting to go into the academy. Capt. Baldy Velasco was the communications commander at the time. One day I was called into Capt. Velasco's office. I was pretty nervous because I wasn't told what this was about. I was a few weeks from going into the academy and the last thing I needed was trouble.

The captain was sitting at his desk with a few teletypes spread out before him. He pointed to the teletypes and said, "What is this Don"? I was standing in front of his desk, so I leaned over to get a look at what he was talking about.

As I did so, my tie dipped down into the captain's coffee cup. I straighten up and did the only thing I knew to do. I grabbed the bottom of my tie and rung the coffee out of my tie back into the captain's coffee cup.

The captain looked at me, shook his head, and without a word motioned towards the door. For days, I sweated blood fearing the worst, but nothing was ever said, nothing about the teletypes or the captains coffee.

I later entered the academy and to this day, I do not know what the captain wanted to show me.

Ollie Bond

Greg Eavenson #680

My first 4 years I patrolled from Ehrenberg to the Maricopa county line on I-10 & US60. I-10 ran from MP 1 to MP 30 then traffic had to divert onto US60. During my first 6 months we had good radio coverage in 1970 while in District 4. But in January '71 area 4.4 became area 1.5 out of Kingman and radio problems became common place. Kingman dispatch could broadcast/ receive on KDZ424 near Salome or KLM753 north of Parker. My first conversation with Kingman dispatch came on my return from Yuma in-service training. It was about 2100 hours when I called "544 Kingman ". A gruff voice answered "544 what tower are you on"? I replied "Maybe KFX373" and the gruff voice said "I don't have one of those on my console but I do have KLM753". "Ok" I said, "We're on 753." The gruff voice asked "Well what do you want 544?" I replied, "Crossing into California now sir". The voice came back sharply "I'm not a SIR I'm a MAAM!" My first conversation with Ollie Bond. What a great lady.

Anyway the radio was always going down, so we depended on motorists flagging us down or help from Danny Nasca at Ramsey's Ghost Town

Towing. We would try to drive past his place at MP 34.5 every 30 minutes. If dispatch needed us Danny would tie a white rag to his wrecker antenna, and we would stop and call on the phone. If it was a 961 or worse Danny would come find us in his wrecker.
Danny Nasca was a true friend to all law enforcement.

He's In The Trunk

Jim Davis #734

I was working an evening shift on US60 south of Wickenburg and just North of Morristown . I was south bound when I noticed an old pickup N/B come around a curve and almost run off the road. I turned across at the next access and started after it. He wasn't going too fast and was using both lanes to drive in. I finally got the pickup stopped just north of MP114.

I started to talk to the driver and he was obviously intoxicated. I got him out of the pickup and he was filthy and he had obviously crapped his pants and he was ripe. I walked him to the back of my patrol car (1974 Mercury Monterey) and opened the trunk. I kept an old blanket in there, so I spread it out and then maneuvered him so he faced me, I then GENTLY pushed him and he fell into the trunk compartment. There was no way he was going to ride in the inside of my new car.

I then proceeded to the Wickenburg Police/MCSO Jail. I drove up and Deputy Howard Grace was working the desk that night . I went in and told him I had a prisoner to book . Howard looked out the window and said he must of escaped I don't see any one in the car. I told him he was in the car but you can't see him. I told Howard to follow me as I was going need some help getting him out of the car . We went out to the car and I popped the trunk and Howard busted out laughing ,so I told him the reason he was in the trunk . We got him out and walked him to the outside cell block where he was then stripped to the bare skin and given a shower with the garden hose the trusties used to wash the squad cars.

So ended on of my most memorable times in Wickenburg.

Let's Get A Clown

Bob Ticer #4490

I remember the date clearly, October 31, 1993-Halloween. Not only was it Halloween, it was the birthday of the rookie that I was training that evening, Officer Jim Congrove #4776. Jim picked me up at my residence in Prescott Valley just before 1600 hours to start our shift. Officer Congrove being the excellent student that he was, provided me with the paperwork from his previous night's arrests and crash reports. Jim still complains that I "made" him write his reports on his off time during FTO. Of course I did, times have surely changed, but that is another story. Back to Halloween…

Once we left my residence, we had a five minute ride to State Route 69 to start working traffic. While Jim drove, I told him that I wanted him to arrest a clown for DUI during the shift since it was Halloween. Jim, again being the fine student that he was, agreed to the request. As we approached the highway from Prescott East Highway, we both noticed the vehicle in front of us bump into a raised curb with the passenger tires. I said, "there you go." Jim lit the suspected drunk driver up for the violation. Once the driver pulled to the right, Jim walked up and contacted the driver, while I hung back near the right rear of the vehicle. A minute or so later, Jim walked back to me and said, "He's drunk." I said, "Excellent Officer Congrove, is he a clown?" The new patrolman said, "No, but he is dressed just up like Alice Cooper." I said, "Good enough!"

We booked the Alice Cooper look-alike after he blew somewhere around a .17 and still had time for dinner and another drunk or two that celebratory evening. That was the start of a great 25-year career for Officer Congrove and a long-lasting friendship between the two of us.

Bad Guys Say Strange Things On The Phone

Dennis McNulty #1959

I started working vehicle theft investigations in 1989 with the original VTI, then a kind of a stepchild group that was part of the Special Service Division. In 1997 the State Vehicle Task Force was formed which we were folded into. It was and still is a multi-agency task force which had the manpower to attack a common problem all over the state. This also included our own assigned prosecutors to take all of our cases.

Early on we were chasing a meth head who was a prolific Honda thief who loved getting into pursuits with police. He would invariably wreck the stolen or ram a police unit and then flee on foot. He knew that he was a prime target of the task force.

One day he called our stolen vehicle tip phone, identified himself by name and threatened to find out where the DPS detectives chasing him lived. He said he would go to their houses and kill their wives, children and pets. We caught him about a week later and he cried all the way to the Maricopa Sheriff's Office jail.

Later he accepted a plea deal for multiple felonies. At his sentencing hearing our prosecutor played a copy of the recording for the judge. The perp cried even more when the judge gave him the maximum sentence.

About 10 years later I had a case that Avondale PD asked us to take over at the house of a known enforcer for the Mexican Mafia. Turns out he had a small chop shop there with a couple of vin switched stolen cars. During the search of the house we also found drugs and stolen property. He was out on bail after Phoenix PD had arrested him outside of Maricopa County Superior Court. He was part of a plan to attempt to intimidate a county prosecutor who was in trial prosecuting two Mexican Mafia shot callers.

Prior to executing my search warrant my suspect had been transported to a local hospital for a heroin overdose which was the original call Avondale PD had responded to. We located him about a week later and booked him into Maricopa County jail where he was held without bail. Now, whenever a jail inmate makes an outgoing phone call, there is always a recorded warning saying that all jail calls are recorded. My suspect calls a confederate and discusses putting together a plan to put a murder hit out on our task force prosecutor because she charged him with multiple felonies and got him on a no bail hold.

MCSO jail intel detectives immediately placed my suspect in isolation and then put our prosecutor under security protection 24/7.

The suspect later plead guilty to multiple felonies and was given 10 years flat time in the Arizona State Prison. At his sentencing

hearing a recording of his phone call was also played.
Never underestimate the stupidity of wanted people on recorded phones.

Let's Get The Hell Out Of Dodge

Charlie Ruiz #1267

In June1982 the Arizona Department of Public Safety Air Interdiction Unit was routinely checking airports where known drug smugglers who utilized aircraft, either borrowed, stolen or owned, to transport drugs into the United States. One of the aircraft that we were watching was a McDonald Douglas DC7 that was worked on at an old auxiliary air strip south of Chandler, Arizona. This location was used to headquarter slurry bombers that were used during the fire season and were based there for repairs. So, this DC7 fit right into the location which was located on the Gila River Indian Reservation.
The squad, supervised by sergeant Bill Roller, was assigned different airports to check for activity and gather intelligence on smuggling crew's and aircraft.
T & G Airport located on the Gila River Indian Reservation was assigned to agent Mike Stevens and myself. Mike is what I consider the air smuggling expert. I learned so much from Mike, for example he could tell what kind of aircraft landed on a clandestine airstrip by measuring the

wheel base of the plane center to center by the tire prints left on the dirt.

Around June 1982 I was on a routine check of T & G Aviation and as I was driving down the road I noticed some activity around the DC7. I recognized one of the subjects as a well-known drug smuggler who I will mention as BW from now on. Rumors were that BW, who by the way is a pilot of small aircraft, wanted to learn how to fly and operate a larger aircraft like the DC7.

As I was watching the crew and aircraft, they fired up the engines. The crew boarded the plane and taxied the plane to the main runway and took off flying eastbound. I notified U.S. customs as well as my supervisor. The aircraft eventually landed in Austin, Texas. We notified one of our counterparts who was with Texas Department of Public Safety and lived in Austin to keep watch on the DC-7. He surveilled the aircraft when it landed and confirmed that BW was with the crew. The agent, Bob Nesteroff and another customs agent managed to gather enough information to write a court order to install a transponder on the aircraft, but before they could install the transponder, the DC7 took off heading east again landing in Florida. Before the agents could arrive to install the transponders the aircraft again took off this time landing in the St. Maarten Islands.

Bob Nesteroff and the US customs agent were granted permission to install the transponders outside of U.S. territory. They installed one above the pilot's seat in the cockpit and the other one in the tail section of the DC7. Prior to taking off to their destination the smugglers decided to sweep the plane for bugging equipment, for example transponders. The person doing the sweeping failed to locate either one of the transponders. The pilot sat down in the cockpit control panel and at that time one of the transponders fell from above, almost hitting the pilot on the head. At this time the crew panicked and abandoned the DC 7 for approximately 5 to 6 months.

On November 6, 1982 the smuggling crew returned to the DC7 and swept the plane one more time and again they failed to find the one transponder in the tail section. After they were convinced that the aircraft was clean of any bugs they left the St. Maarten Islands in route to Colombia,

The DC7 was picked up on radar by U.S. customs returning from Columbia heading towards the United States at approximately 8:30 PM. The DC 7 crossed into Louisiana followed by customs where they lost the aircraft around Lake Charles, Louisiana.

After not hearing any new information from Customs our crew decided to call it a day at a proximity 10:00 PM. It was at this point that my partner Mike Stevens said " Let's get the hell out of Dodge". So we left the office and went home.

Ironically when I check on the following morning I was told to pack up for a few days, that I was headed to Dodge City Kansas where apparently the DC-7 had landed.

On January 8th Delbert Salazar from the Drug Enforcement Administration, Arizona DPS pilot Jim Heflin and I boarded the King Air around noon and flew to Dodge City Kansas arriving at 4 PM.

As we were landing, I thought we were coming in to Holbrook Arizona. I have never seen flat country like they have in Kansas. We met with the Kansas investigators and were taken where the DC 7 was processed and unloaded prior to us getting there. It was empty at the time. We climbed on board and noticed that they had 55 gallon barrels to pump oil into the 4 engines using a gasoline pump. I also noticed that they had rubber fuel bladders that they used on their trip from Columbia to Louisiana. Apparently, they were not planning on refueling. The case agent from Kansas told us that there was approximately 20,000 pounds of marijuana on board and supposedly they were supposed to land in Jetmore, Kansas which is 30 miles North of Dodge.

The crew escaped before authorities got to the aircraft and scattered into town. It was a cold morning approximately 1 degree below 0. At least it felt like it. They were eventually caught and taken into custody. This all occurred in the early morning hours. The authorities in Jetmore received a call stating that there was suspicious activity at the old air strip at Jetmore and when they got there, they arrested 2 or 3 other people.

The pilot was found waiting at the bus terminal wearing light clothing. I had the opportunity to talk to him and he told me that he was offered $10,000 to fly the aircraft. He needed the money for an operation. Sadly I found out that he was a WWII veteran flying supplies in the Pacific.

We were taken to Jetmore where we found out that one of the crew members was from Chandler, Arizona.

Enough information was gathered to execute a search warrant at his residence by Customs.

After spending the night in Dodge City we flew back to Phoenix the following day.

The smugglers were all tried and convicted and eventually sentenced to prison terms.

As for BW, he was nowhere to be found! He did provide intelligence later on.

You Had To Be There To Believe It

Brian Frank #1148

One night at about oh dark thirty, I was dispatched to an accident on I-10 at the Gila River Bridge about mile post 173, a normal enough call. Upon arrival I learned that two young men, in their twenties were traveling cross country in a passenger vehicle with one driving and the other asleep in the front passenger's seat, when the diver fell asleep; also a not uncommon event with a 55 mph speed limit at night and on a long trip. With both occupants sleeping, the vehicle drifted left and right striking the bridge guard rails on both sides a number of times, like a pin ball machine so to speak, while rotating 180 degrees and coming to a final resting position in the number one west bound lane with the passenger's door up against the guard rail. Needless to say, that at this point both men are now awake and clearly had no idea of what had just happened, but their first instinct was to get out of the car, which the driver did without any trouble. The passenger climbed out the window, as the vehicle was up against the guard rail. No one was injured, at this point so the accident was a 961, or accident without any injuries, nothing unusual.

As I mentioned earlier, the passenger climbed out the side window, not knowing what had happened let alone where he was, taking his first step OVER the guard rail, and falling at least 25 feet or more into the Gila River, which was dry as a bone. The driver, now realizing that the car was on a bridge ran over to the edge and called out in the darkness to find out if his passenger was okay, only to get the reply that he thought that his back was now injured from the fall and he could not move. Note to reader, his back was not just injured but broken! So hence this was an accident without injury, as the vehicle had stopped moving and no one had been injured. The ambulance arrived but was soon stuck in the sandy river bottom. It looked like it was impossible to get the victim to help. No problem, I had called for the DPS helicopter, and this was clearly something that was right up their alley, so to speak.

When Ranger 28 got over head I explained via radio the situation, and pilot looked it over and said that he could land the bird BETWEEN the two bridge spans, which were 75 or so feet apart! My eyes must have looked like trash can covers when the words came out of his mouth. With the paramedic and ambulance driver attending to the injured man on the ground the pilot landed between the spans in an unlit area with only the light from the helicopter to assist him, loaded up the victim and took off again. Needless to say I was speechless. The tow truck pulled the ambulance out of the sand, hooked up the disabled car and we called it a night…

I forgot to mention that this was maybe 1974 or 75, not long after the DPS helicopter program began and most if not all of our pilots had flown in Vietnam so they had lots of experience. I cannot remember who the pilot was, but that was the best flying that I have seen, and even to this date.

A Little Part of Arizona History

By Jim Heflin #1983

On a Saturday evening in Flagstaff John McKean #217 and I were on an Executive flight with Governor Bruce Babbitt. We were eating dinner when both our pagers went off, instructing us to return to the airport ASAP. The Governor needed to return to Phoenix immediately. Don Barcello #515, the Governor's Security officer, informed us that the DPS officers in Morenci had run out of the necessary supplies, i.e.: tear gas, rubber bullets and other riot control equipment. DPS officers had temporarily evacuated the town of Morenci. That's when it became apparent that King Air(911AZ) 1 AZ was to become a re-supply aircraft to Morenci.

I will never forget when we turned the corner into the DPS hangar area. There were Arizona National Guard deuce and a halfs, and National Guard soldiers headed by a National Guard Colonel. This was when things got really busy. John told me to get into the King Air left seat while the aircraft was being refueled. The next thing I knew, boxes were being loaded into the aircraft. The co-pilot's seat even had a large box strapped into it. Obviously, I realized I was going solo on this flight. Once the aircraft was full of equipment front to back, John closed the door and gave me the signal for startup. Just then, Governor Babbitt, who with the National Guard Colonel, had been watching all this activity since we landed, told John to delay start.

Governor Babbitt approached the King Air and signaled me to open the aircraft window, and it appeared he wanted to communicate something to me. I opened the window and I will never forget what he said; "Remember Jim, tonight you have become a little part of Arizona history."

While the departure from Sky Harbor was uneventful, I must admit this was on my mind, I had flown many flights for the DPS bomb squad, recalling Ed Stock #675 and Dave Audsley #546 talking about static electricity and how it could cause unscheduled detonation. Great!!

Normal route of flight was up over Globe and down the valley to Three Points airport. It wasn't hard to locate Morenci as the fires were visible from 50 miles out. I was told later a lot of the fires were caused by truck tires being set on fire. Upon landing, my thought was, I sure hope there is somebody there who knows how to open the aircraft door, because I sure couldn't get to it. Fortunately, a DPS Ranger helicopter was there and I believe it was Duke Moore #1045 who operated the door. Once the aircraft was unloaded, my departure was routine, but as I turned west, toward Phoenix, Morenci was on the right side of the aircraft, the many fires and smoke from the burning tires covering much of the valley, made the scene look surreal. Just another Morenci story.

This One Has Stayed With Me

Dick Lewis #176

Working in the area of Globe during the 60's was really an experience. We had the miners working full blast, the reservations north and east of us and the lakes. US60 and 70 were heavily travelled, so there was a lot going on.

I've been called out to go to a wreck and found a more serious one while I was enroute. The wrecks in the night seem to be the most serious ones.

I was sent one night to an accident just to the east side of the Top Of The World, on a downgrade towards Miami on US60.

When I arrived there was a semi parked westbound in the road on the upgrade, across from the wreck.

I found a sedan on its side off the road. It had been eastbound towards Pinto Creek and had run off the right side of the road. Typical of a driver who fell asleep and ran off the road. This vehicle had run head-on into some large boulders and turned onto its right side.

Inside the vehicle in the front seat were the bodies of a young man and woman. The man had obviously been the driver. The rear seat was a jumble of belongings and clothing. A diaper pail had over turned and had soaked everything. This indicated that there was a child involved, but there was none visible.

During this time, Sgt Snedigar had arrived to assist. We moved some of the clothing in the back seat, and just as we suspected, there was a girl child less than a year old, deceased. She had probably been asleep in the back seat! It is unknown if she had suffocated or died during the collision.

In the semi-truck that was parked on the road was a child (boy) less than three years old. The truck driver had found him alive in the car and took him to safety in the truck.

The most pitiful thing I have ever seen was this little boy looking at me in wonderment. He was not emotional because he didn't know what was going on. His left eye was blackened and was almost swollen shut. No other obvious injury.

I was so stricken that his entire family was across the road dead and that he was so helpless and alone and he had no idea what had happened to him.

My heart went out to this little guy. My brother who was a sergeant with the Gila County Sheriff's Office arrived just as I was climbing down out of the truck. One look at me and he asked me if everything was OK. I told him everything was fine. He later told me that he had never seen such a look on my face before. I still get very emotional recalling the event. Just another day.

I believe that I have been to 2,500 wrecks throughout the state during my 25-year tour of duty. I investigated 67 wrecks in one year during this time in Globe! As a sergeant I attended a lot of them but didn't investigate all of them.

Just Me Talking

Dick Lewis #176

Before the end of the 60's, all we had was Red Cross First Aid training and a small first aid kit. There was no box in the back of the car, no extinguishers.

In Globe we had no ambulance. The mortuary sent out their hearse and a driver with no training. I have used anything I could for splints, etc.

Martin Luther King and the Vietnam war improved a lot of things that we needed to do our job. Like, new improved radio service, night sticks, shotguns, pay raises, helicopters, ambulances, paramedics and a lot more.

One thing that I have come to realize from writing these stories is that there are many of our experiences that we can't re-tell for some reason or the other. I also have more than ever come to realize that there were and are more than one of us out there being exposed to the world of emergencies, heart break and joy. It seems that I was alone in the dark at the end of the road helping where I could, with little or no recognition. I believe we saved lives every day, whereas a fireman makes the front page and gets an award, which is good, but that's just the way it is.

The attention that PTSD is a result of what our servicemen encounter has come to realize it happens to first responders also, even if it is 40 years later! That's what the experts say.

Out Of Gas

Bob Ticer #4490

We all know about the policy that requires a highway patrolman to fill up their patrol car with fuel at the end of the shift… Well, I had a long shift (or some other excuse), and I didn't fill up my tank before I went home back when I was a young officer stationed out of Cordes Junction, and you guessed it, the phone rang about 0200 hours, waking me up out of a deep sleep. One of our fine dispatchers out of Flagstaff said, "Officer Ticer we have a fatal at milepost 268 northbound I-17 in the median." I quickly put my jump suit on and headed out the door to my patrol car for the quick trip north. Upon arrival, I found that a drunk driver ran straight through the end of a guardrail in the median where the roadway curved, quickly killing him. After my sergeant completed some photos and assisted me with measuring the crash, he left me with the mortuary and arriving tow truck to finish up the scene.

Just as the tow truck driver was completing his work, my patrol car ran out of gas. I only had one option and that was to humbly ask the driver if he could spot me some fuel. He said, "Ticer, don't you have a policy about filling up at the end of your shift." I just looked at him and said, "just a couple gallons please and don't tell anyone about this." For $5.00 he loaned me some gas to make it back home. The next day, when back on shift, I stopped at the tow yard in Mayer to catch up with my "friends" the tow truck drivers. As soon as I stepped out of the car, one of them said, "Hey, I heard you ran out of gas last night, I thought you had a policy against that." I turned around, got back in my car, and went out to write tickets for the rest of my shift and made sure I filled up in the future. I can still hear them laughing to this day.

Laid Back Radar

Johnny Sanchez #1463

It was the summer of I believe around 1978 and our motor squad supervised by Chuck McCarty was assigned to work a speed/truck detail on west I-8 outside of Yuma. Being 100+ degrees out that day we worked a late afternoon shift. Myself, Dave Johnson 689, Larry Jensen 819, Rick Williams 897 and a couple of other motor officers were running radar on the west bound lanes when we saw a lawn chair on the side of the road. Well as you can imagine that seemed like a good place to stretch out and relax a bit since we were way out of town with little traffic. Dave and myself were tempted and kept riding, but Larry Jensen decided to try out the lawn chair while shooting some radar west bound calling the vehicles to us. As luck would have it Chuck McCarty's voice came over the radio in a very mad tone wanting to meet all of us alongside the road. During the major ass chewing he advised us that the Director had been traveling west bound, passing Larry Jensen's location where he was laying on the lawn chair shooting radar and he wanted this situation corrected immediately.

Highway Patrol Wisdom

Paul Palmer #342

Do not give a breathalyzer to a man with a mouthful of tobacco.
Once a woman begins to physically fight you, she becomes a man.
After you fight a suspect and roll around on the ground with him, do not tell him to watch his head when you put him in the backseat of your patrol car.
Never miss a chance to appreciate a happy drunk. It will make up for the mean obnoxious ones you have to deal with.
Your sergeant will always hold a surprise inspection the day before your scheduled barber shop appointment.
Never eat a chili dog while you are driving. A chili dog has a way of finding every bump in the road.

A lady with a flat tire will be your first contact the day you put on a fresh uniform.
The dispatcher will run a code 20 check on you the minute you leave your assigned patrol area.
Strive for promotions, but never become a manager. Become a leader.
Just because a new gadget comes out on the market does not mean you have to hang it on your gun belt.
You may be a Colonel now, but never forget that you were once a patrolman.
Go out of your way to talk to children. It will make future officer's jobs a lot easier.
Your Sergeant doesn't have ESP. When he was a patrolman, he was trying to get away with the same things you are trying to get away with now.
All too often a change in upper management is like rotating four bald tires.
A mustache won't make you look older. It will only cause your lip to itch.
The same man who cusses you when you give him a ticket will be the first to beg for your help when he is in trouble.
No matter how much you complain, you are still with the finest law enforcement agency in the nation and your fellow officers will be some of the closest friends you will ever have. Enjoy yourself. Time goes by way too fast.

Ingram Content Group UK Ltd.
Milton Keynes UK
UKHW021049080523
421393UK00010B/86